Ancient
EGYPTIAN
Holidays

Ancient EGYPTIAN Holidays

Mab Borden

The Witches' Almanac
Providence, Rhode Island

Address all inquiries and information to
THE WITCHES' ALMANAC, LTD.
P.O. Box 25239
Providence, RI 02905-7700

Softcover:
13-ISBN: 978-1-938918-98-8
eBook
978-1-881098-05-8

First Printing February 2024

Printed in USA

1 2 3 4 5 6 7 8 9 10

The land of the desert belongeth by right the son of Nut, and the Two Lands have contentment in making him to rise upon the throne of his father like Ra.

Thou rollest up into the horizon, thou settest the light above the darkness, thou illuminest [the Two Lands] with the light from thy two plumes, thou floodest the Two Lands like the Disk at the beginning of the dawn.

—Hymn to Osiris
translated by Wallis Budge, 1912

Table of Contents

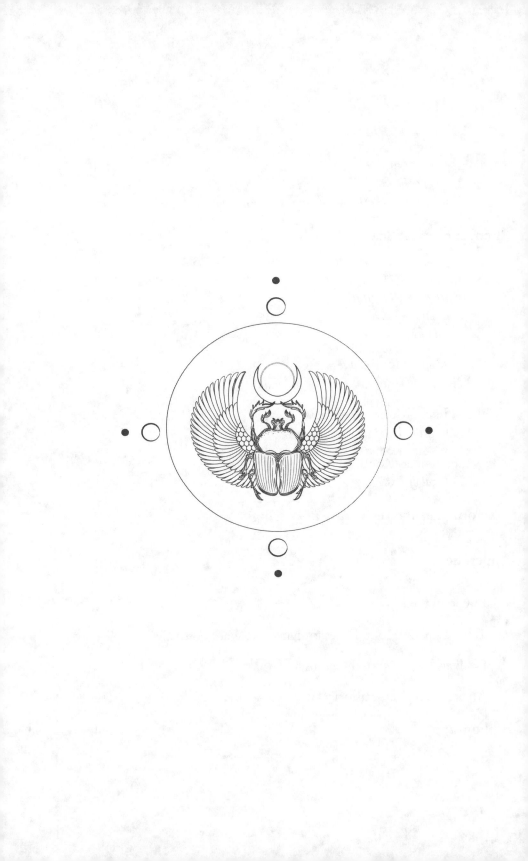

Introduction

As the river rises and falls, Egypt flows through her seasons and Tehuti (Thoth) marks each heb (festival) with a notch on his staff of time. Kemet—Egypt, the Black Land—exists because of the flood and the rich, black soil it leaves in its wake, the sharp flood line marking the boundary between the unforgiving desert and the fertile land. Before the opening of the Aswan Low Dam in 1902 and the Aswan High Dam in 1970, the agricultural rhythm followed the Nile's flood cycle. In ancient times, the cycle of seasons and festivals turned around it as well.

The seasons of ancient Egypt were three and this book is structured around them. First was Akhet, the appearance of the flood waters in late July, which was immediately preceded and annually foretold by the rising of Sirius. The months of Akhet corresponded roughly to the period from the middle of July through the middle of November. After the waters receded was the season of growth, Peret. Crops were sown and tended in the newly fecund fields. This season began in mid-November and continued through mid-March. Egypt is in the Northern hemisphere but the intense heat of the Sahara region necessitates that Winter rather than Summer is the period of growth. Last was Shemu, the harvest season as the Summer came and fields dried out in the desert Sun. This season began in mid-March and continued until mid-July. At the end of the year was the unlucky in-between time of the intercalary epagomenae—the five days added at end of year. These are the days which Nut won by gambling with the Moon so that she could birth the Gods despite being cursed to give birth on no day of the year.

Because the Egyptian calendar was exactly 365 days and did not employ leap years, over time the calendrical months drifted away from the seasons of the flood cycle, so these festivals would have shifted by a day every four years. Over the thousands of years of ancient Egyptian civilization, that made for a considerable dislocation! The date of a specific festival in Gregorian time would be at very different times of year in different eras. For this reason, this book gives dates according to the original Egyptian calendar, which had the first day of the first month on the date of the rising of Sirius, an astronomical event that very closely aligns with the inundation. The current rising of Sirius in Egypt occurs on July 19th, so the first day of the first month of Akhet is set to that day.

Each season has four months and each month was originally named numerically, i.e. "the first month of Akhet," but individual month names developed over time based on the festivals in or near the month. These names changed through the eras of Egyptian history, with distinct Middle Kingdom, New Kingdom, Hellenized and Coptic forms.

MYTHIC CYCLES, DIVINE BEINGS AND FESTIVALS

Each night the Sun and the Sun God Ra sink into the chaos of the underworld—the *Duat*. This realm is ruled by Apophis, the great snake who fights against the Gods. In the battle, Ra is the ram, the falcon, the scarab and all his other forms and many other Gods fight at his side. Every morning he rises triumphant as Khepri, sailing his Boat of Millions of Years across the heavens. He is the upholder of *Ma'at*—truth and order—and his light brings life and warmth as well as reassurance that chaos is still held at bay and the world is still as it should be. This solar cycle upholds the order of creation and the other mythic cycles of creation and the death and kingship of Osiris interact directly with it.

Netjeru (singular *netjer*) is an umbrella term for divine beings that includes the Gods, kings, sacred animals and the dead. Rituals around the dead tend to focus on linking them to various mythic and cosmic cycles, thereby extending the divinity of the netjeru to the dead person so that they may endure in some form.

Egyptian religion generally tended to be temple focused. This did not render it inaccessible to the average person, though. Temples were not run in secret and their priests generally did not wield enormous occult and political power—despite conventions of film and literature that would imply otherwise. In fact, temples employed vast numbers of citizens and served as major economic engines. Festivals were exuberant public affairs that enjoyed broad participation and of course shifted over the many centuries of ancient Egyptian religious practice. Some aspects of Egyptian festivals appear to predate the unification of Upper and Lower Egypt. For example, there is archaeological evidence of possible sacrifice and feasting at Hierakonopolis as early as 3500 BCE.

Festivals could be national, but tended to be regional. There were a handful of major festivals—Wepet-renpet, Wag, Opet, Khoiak,

Nehebkau, Min and the Beautiful Feast of the Valley—but most were lesser and many are known only by their names which appear in lists on temple walls and on work dockets in tombs.

It is extremely important to understand that Egyptian mythology is not neat and the Gods frequently overlap one another in their symbols, titles, functions and names, even in the same region and period. Literal and mythological truth are different creatures, so apparent conflict did not result in any conflict at all. In ancient Egypt, meaning was always additive, so of course Renenutet and Wadjet can both be the uraeus—the cobra on the king's crown. There was no cognitive dissonance for Egyptians in multiple Goddesses being the Eye of Ra or the mother of the same divine child while still being utterly themselves and no other. This is not self-contradiction but rather reflects the rich meaning of the symbols and stories themselves that so many Gods could embody them.

A NOTE ON INTENTIONS AND METHODS

This text is intended to inform and inspire Witches and Pagans of all kinds. It should be noted that the source material is entirely academic, does not draw on the work of the Kemetic reconstructionist communities and that these pages contain no ritual scripts. Anyone looking to resurrect the religious practices of an ancient culture will find that there are always gaps in the historical record, even in a culture with the vast textual and artistic sources of ancient Egypt. Understanding an ancient festival is one thing—enacting it on the other side of the world thousands of years later with incomplete information is another entirely. When faced with the practical logistics of ritual, there are many choices to make and reconstructionist communities have typically spent many years determining what works best for their situations based on what information is available about a given ritual, their broad understanding of the ancient culture, knowledge gleaned from their personal work with the deities in question and what they are able to execute with their particular constraints of time and space. This book is not intended to be a replacement for the deep work of these communities but rather a source of information about the holidays themselves, to be used in any context the reader wishes.

What is presented here is strictly information about each ancient festival, with minimal suggestions for how a modern person might begin to go about honoring each, based on the ancient sources only and not on modern Pagan conventions. Anyone who finds that the material presented resonates with them so much that they desire to deepen their religious practice through regular worship of the Gods of Egypt is encouraged to seek out Kemetic resources in your area and online, as they will be your best guide for further work.

Gregorian Festival Dates

The calendar currently used by most of the world is the Gregorian calendar. The dates provided here are based on the Gregorian date of the Egyptian calendar's original marker, the rising of Sirius on July 19th. The Egyptian calendar drifted considerably in ancient times, though. If you prefer to focus on the agricultural aspects of the seasonal celebrations, you might consider reorganizing them around your local climate. For example, while you can celebrate Khoiak—a pre-ploughing holiday commemorating the death and rejuvenation of Osiris—from a purely mythological standpoint, you could emphasize the agricultural aspects of the holiday such as burying figurines of the God and planting bulbs by celebrating in early Spring in your own region. Of course, celebrating on the traditional dates is respectful to the ancestors—those millions of people over thousands of years who developed these holidays—and these are the dates given below.

July 19: Wepet-renpet Festival
August 5: Wag Festival
August 6: Wag and Thoth Festival
August 7: Tekh, The Feast of Drunkenness
August 9: Procession of Osiris
August 22: Festival of Osiris and the Ennead
September 1–12: Opet Festival
September 22: Feast of Isis, Evening Offerings for Taking the River
September 23: Taking the River
October 3: Lamentations of Isis and Nephthys
October 7: Festival of Ma'at
October 17: Festival of Hathor
November 3: Khoiak Festival Opening
November 7: Khoiak: Ploughing the Earth
November 11: Khoiak: Sokar Festival
November 15: Khoiak: Raising the Djed Pillar
November 16: Feast of Nehebkau, the Beginning of Eternity
December 14: Raising the Willow
January 14: Amun in the Festival of Raising Heaven
January 15: Festival of Ptah, Return of the Statue of Amun
February 17: Day of Chewing Onions for Bast
March 10: Harvest Offerings to Renenutet
March 12: Granary Offerings to Renenutet
March 16: Festival of Renenutet and Birthday of Nepri
March 25: Adoration of Anubis
New Moon in Khonsu: Feast of Min (4 days)
New Moon in Khentkhety: Wadi, the Beautiful Feast of the Valley
May 27: Neith, the Festival of the Lamps

May 29: Offerings to Hapi and Amun to Secure a Good Flood
June 15: Festival of Isis
July 14–18th: Epagomenae (unlucky intercalary days)

Ancient Egyptian calendar on a wall in
Kom Ombo Temple on the Nile, Egypt.

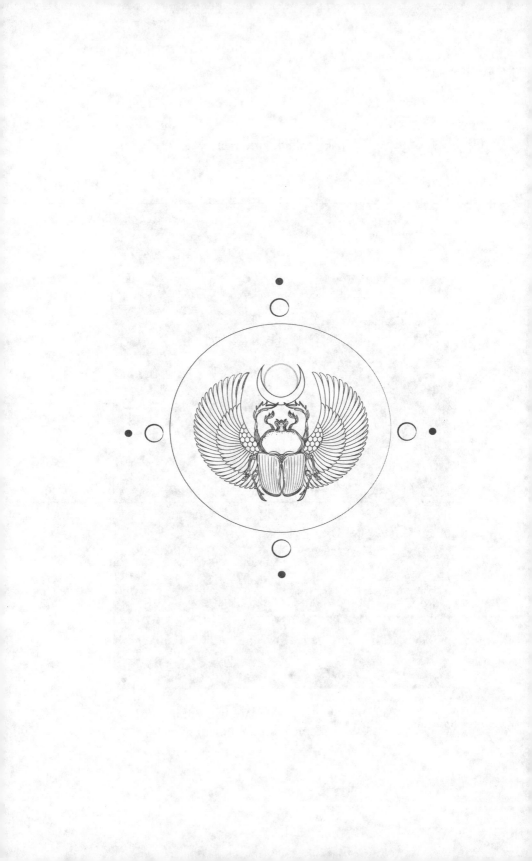

Akhet–Season of the Flood

A	*khet* means appearance, and it begins with that dramatic signal of renewal—the rising river waters. This season includes the following months:

Thoth	July 19–August 17
Menkhet	August 18–September 16
Hathor	September 17–October 16
Khoiak	October 17–November 15

The month of Thoth begins with the new year's celebration of Wepet-renpet and it is the first of many festivals in Akhet. While there are numerous holidays throughout the year, half of the major festivals occur during this season, with the rest spread across the growing and harvest seasons.

The *netjer* (God) of the season is Hapi, the God of the Flood. While there is no single personification of the Nile, Hapi represents the river in its life-giving inundation stage. The prayer below is excerpted from Oliver Thatcher's 1907 translation of the 2100 BCE *Hymn to the Nile*. The full text mentions sacrificing birds and gazelles as well as burning men, presumably all as offerings to the God. Southern Egypt could go many years without any rainfall at all and Egyptian agriculture and survival depended entirely on the annual flood. While the ancient Egyptians were aware of Ethiopia, they were not familiar with its melting snows and heavy mountain rains that cause the inundation. Indeed, even when a source of largesse is fully known, it can still be unreliable—as anyone who's had a paycheck lost in the mail knows! Then when relief comes, it feels like a miracle. Similarly, this prayer emphasizes Hapi's nature as predictable yet

Hapi presenting the gifts of the river.

mysterious, benevolent yet capable of withholding his gifts. In his annual rhythm, Hapi at once supported the life of Egypt and served as reminder of just how precarious that life could be.

Prayer to the Netjer of the season
Hail to thee, O Nile!
Mysterious is thy issuing forth from the darkness
on this day whereon it is celebrated!
Watering the orchards created by Re,
to cause all the cattle to live,
You give the Earth to drink, Inexhaustible One!

Lord of the Fish, during the inundation
no bird alights on the crops.
You create the grain, you bring forth the barley,
assuring perpetuity to the temples.
If you cease your toil and your work, then all
that exists is in anguish.
If the Gods suffer in heaven, then the faces
of men waste away.

But all is changed for mankind when he comes.
He is endowed with the qualities of Nun.
If he shines, the Earth is joyous, every stomach
is full of rejoicing, every spine is happy, every
jawbone crushes its food.

He brings the offerings, as chief of provisioning.
He is the creator of all good things as
Master of Energy, full of sweetness in his choice.
He brings forth the herbage for the flocks

and sees that each God receives his sacrifices.
He spreads himself over Egypt, filling the
granaries, renewing the marts, watching
over the goods of the unhappy.

He is prosperous to the height of all
desires, without fatiguing Himself therefor.
He is not sculptured in stone.
In the statutes crowned with the uraeus
serpent, he cannot be contemplated.
None knows the place where he dwells,
none discovers his retreat by the power
of a written spell.

No dwelling is there which may contain you!
None penetrates within your heart!
He stanches the water from all eyes and watches
over the increase of his good things.

Where misery existed, joy manifests
itself—all beasts rejoice.
He makes mankind valiant, enriching some,
bestowing his love on others.

He shines when he issues forth from
the darkness to cause his flocks to prosper.
It is his force that gives existence to all
things—nothing remains hidden for him.
He watches over his works, producing the
inundation during the night.

Night remains silent, but all is changed by the
inundation—it is a healing balm for all mankind.
Establisher of justice! Mankind desires you,
supplicating you to answer their prayers.
You answer them by the inundation! Men offer
the first fruits of corn. All the Gods adore you!
But we are not nourished on lapis lazuli—wheat
alone gives vigor.

When you shine in the royal city, the rich
man is sated with good things.
The poor man even disdains the lotus. All that is
produced is of the choicest.
All the plants exist for your children.

If you have refused nourishment,
the dwelling is silent.
Devoid of all that is good, the country
falls exhausted.
O inundation of the Nile, offerings are made
unto you, great festivals are instituted for you.
The God manifests not his forms,
he baffles all conception.

Come and prosper! Come and prosper!
O Nile, come and prosper!
O you who make men to live through his flocks
and his flocks through his orchards!
Come and prosper, come, O Nile, come
and prosper!

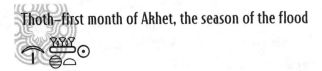

Thoth—first month of Akhet, the season of the flood

July 19–August 17

After the rising of Sopdet—the star called Sirius in modern times—the flood waters came and the ancient month of Thoth began. Egypt is Kemet, the Black Land, the fertile fields in the midst of the desert. But Kemet's soil returns quickly to dust without the water and silt gifted each year by the Nile's flood. You do not need to live in a place that floods to experience the joy of the Opening of the Year, however! The relief and renewal this month brings is not limited to the agricultural cycle. In fact, since the completion of the Aswan dam in 1970 the Nile no longer floods the fields of Egypt—nonetheless she remains the lifeblood of the land. Likewise, you can celebrate the festivals that occur in Thoth and honor their *netjeru* (Gods and divine spirits) regardless of your seasonal or agricultural circumstances.

There are quite a few festivals in this month, beginning with the Opening of the Year on the first day of the month. Consider making offerings to Thoth as the netjer of the month and to Hapi as the netjer of the season. Take note of the following dates:

> *1st of the month—July 19th*: Wepet-renpet festival,
>   the Opening of the Year.
> *18th of the month—August 5*: Wag Festival
> *19th of the month—August 6* Wag and Thoth Festival
> *20th of the month—August 7*: Tekh, the Feast of Drunkenness
> *22nd of the month—August 9*: Procession of Osiris

WEPET-RENPET, THE OPENING OF THE YEAR

The first dawn of creation is described in a hymn from the New

Kingdom as making the sky like gold and the waters like lapis lazuli. Each flood is a new birth of the world—may each first dawn be just as beautiful. Since the Nile has not flooded in fifty years, celebrate this festival on July 19th, which corresponds to the first day of Thoth, the first month in the Egyptian year. And be sure not to forget Tentruty in your offerings—she is the ancestress in whose *Book of the Dead* the Lamentations and accompanying instructions survived to modern times.

⊛

Before the world was born, before even the Gods, there was *Nun*, primordial water. A mound—the *benben*—rose out of it and that mound became Egypt. By what magic was it formed? Atum created himself and then formed the other Gods. Ptah made Atum with just words and will. Amun-Ra created the Gods from his sweat and people from his tears. A bird's call broke the silence of chaos. In the form of a scarab, Ra came forth from a lotus. Khnum spun the world into being on his potter's wheel. The mystery is too beautiful for a single story! Egypt is rich with tales of how the world of Gods and humans came to be and the waters remain a constant through them all just as they remained a constant in ancient Egyptian life. With each new year's inundation, Nun returned, the Nile washing over temple thresholds, bringing life and threatening death. With each renewal of this cycle, Egypt became again the benben, that earliest first version of herself reaching up to seize the potential of her being as something independent of the chaos that birthed her.

The festival of Wepet-renpet was movable, beginning when the river waters rose in the flood. Originating late in the Old Kingdom period, it was marked by feasting and celebration. Egyptians celebrated some of these feasts in the courtyards of tombs, graves rising as their own benbens like the pyramids of the great kings.

Osiris the dead king rules forever, enthroned in the under-world realm of the *Duat*. Death brings life and so the murdered king's mummy is green as his very body contributes itself to the Nile and through it to the land. Remember him and call him to the feast! As a bull he waits, and the back and forth rhythms of the *Lamentations of Isis and Nephthys* always reach his ears and stir his heart.

Two women sit alone on the ground in the temple, in the doorway of the hall where the God will appear. The names are written on them: Isis and Nephthys, the throne and the pylon drawn clear on their arms. With bowed heads they hold blue-glazed jars of water in their right hands, loaves of bread in their left. The beloved sisters of Osiris call him, their voices rising over the tambourines.

> Come to your house! Come to your house!
> Your sisters long to see you!
> Come to your house! Come to your house!
> Great king, whose enemy has fallen,
> You shine for us like the sun!
> Our hearts are lightened to see you,
> your beloved sisters' hearts are glad!
> Nothing evil can come to the one
> whose eyes rest on your face!
> You rise and set as Sah—Orion,
> I follow as Sopdet—Sirius!
> I keep your feasts and remember you!
> I follow as Sopdet forever and
> do not depart from Sah!
> The bull who is lover, come to your house!
> Come see your mother, come see your sisters,
> my brother my son!

Come see your son Horus,
see Horus give you offerings!
For your ka your sisters pour out water.
Your son gives bread, beer, meat and fowl.
Thoth himself recites your prayers and
calls you with spells!

Before you the Gods pour out offerings!
Come to your house, Great King!
Come to your house, Wsjr, and do not depart!
Oh, he comes!

WAG, A FEAST OF OSIRIS TO HONOR THE DEAD

Originally a lunar festival that shifted date, Wag was incorporated into the civic calendar on the 18th day of Thoth. This can be modernized to August 5. It was not a strictly temple-based occasion and was celebrated by individuals as well as by priests. It is one of the oldest Egyptian festivals.

❁

The people and priests of Egypt made paper shrines, paper boats for all the things that had passed. Even the Great King dies and there has never been any person or God whose time will not come. They made boars for *Wsjr*—Osiris. They made boats for their ancestors who are Osiris now. They placed some on graves and when darkness fell they took others to the river. They pointed them West to the place of death, to the desert where the kings still lay in their stone sepulchers. They pointed them to follow the path of the Sun so the ancestors may rise and set with Ra forever.

Wsjr's body leaks from his tomb, spilling life over Egypt. He is Wenenefer, the one whose body does not decay. A wall of fire surrounds his corpse in Rosetau, but the river is flowing with his sweat, his seed and his putrefaction. The ancestors' life spills through him because they are Osiris now. You will rise with the river, too, some day.

The priests and people of Egypt stepped down into the Nile waters on the eastern side where life rules. They called out the names of the ones they loved. They called the ancestors and Osiris and then set the boats to sail. A thousand paper boats crossed by night, crossed the river to their judgment. Ten thousand boats for ten thousand souls, how many thousand nights in how many thousand years? All things die and may they all become Osiris and rule in the Duat forever.

Osiris is the emmer and the barley rising from the green Earth. The sustenance of the people, Osiris the Great King is dead and he rules with crook and flail. His skin is green because his body returns to the water. His skin is black because the land is fertile. When *Mesektet* the night boat carries Ra to the cavern where Wsjr's body lays, in the darkest hour Ra becomes Wsjr—Osiris—and all live on.

WAG AND THOTH FESTIVAL OF OSIRIS AND THOTH

Over time, the Wag Festival became associated with Thoth as well as Osiris. The 19th day of the month of Thoth was devoted to both these Gods.

✵

One of Egypt's oldest netjeru, Thoth appeared in the first dynasty as a baboon with a dog's head. His association with the ibis began in the Old Kingdom and by late periods Thoth was consistently depicted with the head of an ibis, although baboon statues still appeared even in Roman times. He wears the crescent Moon among other crowns and typically holds a palette and a pen to denote his dominion over writing. The Scribe God was lord of all secret arts and ruled over the lunar phases and the stars, and by extension the seasons, astronomy, math and science. He and Horus together libate kings both living and dead. Thoth records Osiris' verdicts over souls in the Hall of the Judgement and when Ma'at is personified as a Goddess, Thoth is her husband. He upholds rightness and order as a God of wisdom and justice but like the Moon he wears on his brow, he has tricks up his sleeve, too.

One particular story of Thoth aligns strongly with this season of renewal. In this story Tefnut—the personification of moisture—is also the eye of Ra. She and her brother Shu—Air—were so close to Ra in the Nun that all three were like a single being. When they were separated, Tefnut became angry with her father and left Egypt entirely. She traveled South to Nubia—modern Sudan—where she took the form of a lion and laid waste to everything in her sight. The gaze of the eye of Ra is fiery and destructive, even when embodied in a water Goddess. Meanwhile, Egypt was suffering without Tefnut—when she left, she took all the moisture in the country with her.

Tefnut, personification of moisture

No God was equal in strength to the power of Ra's Eye, so Ra sent Thoth to fetch her back through his wits and his words. In the shape of a baboon with the head of a dog, Thoth reminded Tefnut of the duties of a daughter of Ra. He lectured, he scolded, he sermonized to remind her of her dignity. He told her tales of all the suffering that had befallen Egypt without her and reminded her how beloved she was there. He described the songs that would greet her, the incense that would be burned for her, the offerings that awaited if only she would return. Knowing that stories instruct as well as delight, Thoth then began to tell her fables and thus eventually persuaded her to journey back to Egypt with him.

This is one of the stories that moved her heart:

Everyone feared the mighty lion that lived on the mountain—no animal was stronger. One day the lion came upon a panther whose fur had all been pulled out and whose skin was cut in many places. Outraged, the lion asked the panther who had done this to him. "Man," the panther told him. Lion had never seen humans before, but he swore he would find Man and punish him.

Lion left the mountain to find this Man and on the way, he found many animals. He found oxen and horses, donkeys and cows, bears and even another lion. All were in chains or terribly wounded and all told him that Man had tricked them in one way or another to cause their suffering. Lion swore to each that he would find Man and make him pay—blood for blood.

One of the few animals Lion encountered that hadn't been harmed by Man was a small mouse. It had run under Lion's paw without realizing it. Since no mouse could hope to fight or outrun the mighty Lion, it could now only beg for its life, and—like Thoth—use its wits to convince the stronger creature of its case. "I'm very small," said the mouse. "For one like you, I'm not even big enough to make a snack. I'm hardly worth eating, but I am worth keeping alive. If you spare me today, I'll owe you and one day—who knows—I might save your life as well." The lion could not stop laughing at the thought that anyone could ever threaten him so that his life would need saving. In his amusement, he decided to let the mouse go free.

Lion had underestimated the wicked heart and crafty mind of Man, who laid a trap for him. Man dug a pit and spread a net over it. Then he hid it beneath grass and reeds and waited. Lion fell in and was caught. He struggled to get free but it seemed that the more he twisted against the ropes and leather of the net, the tighter the knots became.

When night fell, Lion began to know fear. In the darkest hour, the mouse came to repay his debt. "It is beautiful to do good," the mouse told Lion. He chewed through the net, climbed onto the lion's back and rode in his mane as they returned to the mountains together.

When Tefnut returned with Thoth, the flood returned with her, Ma'at was restored and life could continue. Ra wept when he saw his daughter and his tears were the first humans.

The words for "tears" and "humans" in ancient Egyptian are homophones. In the *Book of the Heavenly Cow* from the New Kingdom, Thoth—ever full of tricks and sly with words—takes on titles and functions that sound quite a bit like the words for "baboon" and "ibis." Thoth is in fact so old that even the meaning of his name is obscure—another mystery he keeps to himself. He has many stories that contradict each other and that is just how he likes it. Beware of trying to limit him—Thoth rules much and will not take to being cornered into a single face or function.

TEKH, THE FEAST OF DRUNKENNESS

The festival of Tekh in honor of Sekhmet and Hathor was on the 20th day of the month of Thoth. Beginning in the Middle Kingdom and revived under Roman rule, this popular feast provided worshippers an opportunity for ecstatic union with the Goddess.

✳

The first morning rays crept over the porch of the temple and began to warm the faces and eyelids of worshippers who had passed out there the night before. Hekats and double-hekats of wine had hardly been enough to calm them and even now the temple drums still beat on. The night rhythm had been as insistent as the lion rage of the Goddess, but this morning it rose and fell like the steps of a joyful dance. Ra's morning warmth—his daily blessing to Kemet—spread into the courtyard. The worshippers began to stir, the love of the joyful Goddess welling up in their hearts and filling their eyes with welcome tears of peace. A night to release all and a morning to fall fully in love with the world: this is why they had come.

The Drunken Goddess

The Sun-God Ra was growing old. He became like a statue: his bones silver, his skin gold and his hair lapis lazuli. People no longer believed in the power of this tired king and when they stopped fearing him, they stopped acting in the ways of order and justice. Some even began to plot against him, intending to overthrow the order of the whole world for their own power and indulgence.

Wise Ra gathered the other primordial Gods in council: Moisture and Air, Earth and Sky, the waters of Nun and his own Eye. On their advice, he decided to send the Eye out into the world to survey, judge and punish the hearts of humankind. Since the first people were tears in the Eye of Ra, it was fitting that the Eye should be the one to smite them. The Eye went out into the world as Hathor.

All the people with guilty hearts fled before her face. They ran to the desert and she struck them down. More and more, she butchered them until she waded in human blood. She overpowered them completely and the slaughter was sweetness in her fierce heart. She returned to Ra at the end of the day and he told her to harvest the guilty as grain, to cull them as a flock. Then Hathor the Eye was Sekhmet the Lioness.

The second day, Sekhmet turned to the fields of Kemet. No blameworthy people ran from her face—she had killed all the wrongdoers—but still Sekhmet massacred them. Ra's heart turned toward humanity in kindness and he set out to stop Sekhmet. As his Eye, her power was his power, so he could not overcome her by force. He had to trick her back into herself.

He ordered his servants to the mines and the breweries. They stained the barley mash with ochre and produced seven thousand jars of beer as red as human blood. On the third day Ra went out before dawn and spilled the beer over the fields, jar after jar until the pools were three hands deep. Sekhmet set out again with the rising sun, her heart set on carnage. The thick, red beer gleaming in the morning light like the blood of battle caught her eye. When she approached, her own fearsome face shined back at her from its surface and she was delighted with her own magnificent beauty. She knelt to lap up the blood and the beer pleased her spirit. Sekhmet stumbled back drunk to the house of Ra and he welcomed her. She woke again as Hathor.

Too weary to go on, Ra could no longer abide the Earth. He left the world to other Gods for safekeeping and set Osiris in charge of humans. Many people cried out to him not to leave but from that time on people had to fight to uphold order, a struggle that still continues. Nut the Sky turned into a cow and Ra rode into the night on her back. When he reached the sky, Ra transformed himself into many stars and constellations. He formed the Fields of Paradise where the souls of the worthy rest at the end of their lives. Those killed on the first day of Sekhmet's rage were enemies of Ra and suffer eternally in the Underworld for their crimes. All who pass through the Duat shudder to hear their cries. Those pure in heart take satisfaction from the suffering of such evil ones and know gladness when the righteous prevail.

Hathor the House of Horus

As his mother, her body was Horus' first dwelling place. Hathor is shown with cows' horns, Sun disks and ostrich plumes, which royalty and other deities also wore. The queen was the first of her priestesses and her temple attendants carried sistrums and wore or carried *menat* necklaces with many beads that made a rattling sound. Hathor was called Mistress of the Stars and the Lady of Contentment. She was Sekhmet as the Eye of Ra.

Sekhmet Who Dances on Blood

She is the divine turned to rage. Both destructive and protective, Sekhmet became associated with the fierce side of several Goddesses, most notably Hathor. A Goddess of medicine, her arrows bring plague but she can also vanquish the demons of disease. Sekhmet stands in the prow of Ra's boat in his nightly journey through the Duat, the Underworld. She defends him and the order he represents from the monstrous chaos of the snake Apophis. May your enemies fall before you as they would before Sekhmet the Great!

Menkhet—second month of Akhet, the season of the flood

August 18th–September 16th

The netjer of the month is Ptah, the architect God of creation and craftsmen. Hapi remains the netjer of the season. Early in the month is a minor feast of Osiris and the Ennead—the nine Gods who were the center of worship in Heliopolis. The Ennead includes and flows outward from Ra-Atum and mirrors early stages of creation and the world. After Atum are his first children Tefnut (moisture) and Shu (Air.) Their children Geb (Earth) and Nut (sky) follow, and then last are Geb and Nut's children Osiris, Isis, Seth and Nephthys.

The major festival in the month of Menkhet is the feast of Opet, which lasts at least eleven days. Take note of the following dates:

5th of the month—August 22: festival of Osiris and the Ennead
15th–26th of the month—September 1–12: Opet festival

OPET

Beginning on the 15th day of Menkhet and lasting at least eleven days and as many as twenty-seven, this Theban festival came to national prominence with the political domination of Thebes in the New Kingdom. It played an important role in connecting the king with Amun, the primary Theban deity. The king played a significant role in the festival, which included his ritual marriage to Amun-Ra. This ensured the king's fertility and by extension the economic and political stability of Egypt.

Amun

The powerful Sun God was Khepri in the morning, Ra at midday and Amun in evening. His name *Amun* means "the hidden one," and during the Middle Kingdom period, he became the primary God of Thebes where he was typically shown as a man with a beard and ostrich plume crown. In later periods he was shown with a ram's head and horns.

By the New Kingdom, Amun was associated with the original creator Sun God and was king of the Gods. He was a divine king and the living king was his son. As self-created God he was always creating and his very presence brought life. His statue would periodically visit the Theban city of the dead where he would breathe life back into the deceased by uniting with Hathor, the Goddess of that necropolis. Egyptian polytheism was not animistic and most Egyptian Gods lived somewhere particular, usually the sky. However, Amun was something of an exception because his spirit could be felt everywhere.

When statues left their shrines they travelled in boats even over land. Travel in ancient Egypt was principally by river so boats were the primary vehicle. Gods—including the nearly omnipresent Amun—lived in the heavens with the Sun and the sky is blue so it only stands to reason that it's made of water, particularly the waters of Nun that surround the world. Amun was accompanied during Opet by his wife Mut and their son, Khonsu—the potter who forms each human body on his wheel. They would travel to meet and become one with Amun-Ra in another temple. Amun's presence is inherently vivifying, so the exponential self-empowerment of the God who gives life giving life to the lifegiver—himself—was an expression of renewal. The king especially benefitted from this, as in this process he was also unified through marriage with the God and became his son. Don't get caught up in the appearance of superficial conflict—the ancient Egyptian mind preferred direct explanations and natural metaphors to abstractions. Theological coherence was not the goal and a kaleidoscope of concepts and imagery was enriching rather than confusing. The important bit for the worshipper was that when Amun's power was magnified by his own presence, the king was stronger, Egypt was stronger and so was the common person.

Temples and priests

The primary feature of the celebration was the procession of the statues of Gods from their temples in Thebes to other temples. The people could seek oracles from the statues and while the line was always long, it was a marvelous party with the state providing bread, beer and sweets for the worshippers. Festivals such as Opet generally reflected the largesse of the state and the temple. Modern festivities can celebrate this spirit of generosity by sharing food and particularly by giving some away without expectation of immediate or personal exchange.

Temples had their own fields and granaries that directly employed thousands of people. In addition, temple offerings were reverted to the priesthood. The Gods did not need to keep offerings for themselves and each of the many priests was entitled to a portion of the year's offerings. Most priesthoods were part-time and even short-term jobs held by ordinary people in addition to their other professions, so temples served as economic engines that stimulated the areas around them.

Participating in even the lowest levels of priesthood would be listed with pride among the accomplishments of a person's life, much in the same way many modern people are proud of their military service at any level. Most priests did not hold a great deal of power or even need to know how to read. While there were levels of priesthood that held great political influence and secret religious knowledge, this was not the case for most.

Oracles

During the festival procession, the boat of Amun was carried by the lowest-ranking priests—the *wabs*—who sensed the movement of the statue for oracles. They were responsible, then, for making it move in response to the questions of worshippers and therefore accepting or rejecting requests. The God's will could move the boat toward or away from the questioner or press on the wabs and make the boat seem heavier. If the prow of the boat tilted forward, the God was assenting to a request. A shaking boat indicated an upset deity. The oracle could appoint officials and even identify criminals. This all happened in public rather than in the dark recesses of the temple. The people might have been passive in this process, but they were all witnesses to everyone's questions. While higher ranking priests interpreted these movements, everyone could see them so the level of politically convenient fudging from the higher ranks would necessarily be limited. The Egyptians were no fools, either—the wabs themselves were not allowed to ask questions. There was a great deal of pageantry, but room for only so much trickery.

To see the God carried forth in his boat must have been a great wonder as ordinary worshippers did not enter temples or witness offerings. The parts of the temples that housed the statues of the Gods were off limits even to most priests. Nonetheless, statues were an important contact point between Gods and humanity and this is part of why Opet was such a significant occasion—the ordinary person could see the statue of the God, could ask him a question and expect a response. When the boat of Amun left the temple, the Hidden God you could always feel could now be seen. Like the breeze, his presence was everywhere but invisible and the procession of the statue in its boat made the God visible, tangible, concentrated into a form and place that the ordinary person could approach.

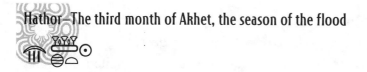

Hathor—The third month of Akhet, the season of the flood

September 17th–October 16th

The netjer of the season is Hapi and the netjer of the month is Hathor. Her festival is at the beginning of the following month, Khoiak. There are no major festivals this month, although the longer Opet festival might at times spill over into Hathor's month. There are several minor feasts worth noting.

> *6th of the month—September 22*: Feast of Isis, evening offerings for Taking the River.
> *7th of the month—September 23rd*: Taking the River
> *17th of the month—October 3*: Lamentations of Isis and Nephthys
> *21st of the month—October 7*: Festival of Ma'at

There is a minor feast of Isis early in the month, although the more significant celebration for this Goddess comes at the end of the year. Evening offerings on that day are associated with the next day's festival, Taking the River. This festival name is recorded on a Middle Kingdom papyrus without elaboration. Ten days later is minor feast for the Lamentations of Isis and Nephthys, which is a fitting time to read the text of the same name aloud.

FESTIVAL OF MA'AT

At the end of the month of Hathor is a feast of Ma'at, the personification of balance, justice and order. This is a festival about which little is known. Ma'at herself is prevalent in mythology and appears in old kingdom art, but her temples are few and don't appear until the New Kingdom. The one at Karnak served as a site for coronation, and the Goddess does not appear to have received offerings there.

In the judgement hall of Osiris after death, an individual's personal morality is judged when the heart is weighed on scales with Ma'at as the counterbalance in the form of a feather. In late periods, she is also shown as a woman with wings that she beats to revive the deceased.

Ma'at is a daughter of Ra, the creator God of the Sun, and she travels with him in his boat through the sky, giving him life. The civilization of the Black Land was maintained against the backdrop of the death-bringing, chaotic desert. It is the role of the king to maintain and promote Ma'at in the realm in his actions as king as well as through his personal uprightness because chaos is a constant threat to the world. This underscores the ruler's connection to the prosperity of the land because Ma'at was also the necessities of life—air, bread and beer. A king whose realm was starving had failed to uphold Ma'at for the realm.

To honor Ma'at in this minor festival, take stock of your actions and your character. Consider yourself in relation to the ideal of Ma'at. How are you upholding order and justice? As king of your own life, are you living in Ma'at so that your house may prosper? What actions can you take to align yourself with Truth? This is not a suggestion to list your failings or lament your limitations, but an opportunity to plan how you can best express and live out the greatest part of your heart. It is beautiful to do good.

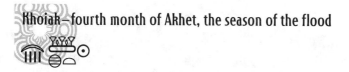

Khoiak—fourth month of Akhet, the season of the flood

October 17th–November 15th

The netjer of the month is Sekhmet—the lioness Eye of Ra—and Hapi is the netjer of the flood season. This month sees the festival of Hathor as well as the great festival of Khoiak for Osiris, a series of feasts and events which could extend nearly to the end of the following month. Regardless of the timing, the Khoiak ceremonies ought to be celebrated in a sequence together. Take note of the following dates:

1st of the month—October 17: Festival of Hathor
18th of the month—November 3: beginning of
    Khoiak Festival
22nd of the month—November 7: Khoiak—Ploughing
    the Earth
26th of the month—November 11: Khoiak—Sokar Festival
30th of the month—November 15: Khoiak—Raising the
    Djed Pillar

FESTIVAL OF HATHOR

This popular festival to celebrate the birth and blessings of Hathor was held at her main cult center at Dendera. Hathor presided over more than twenty-five festivals. At all of them, she is consistently associated with music and dancing, and two of her primary symbols are the sistrum and the menat necklace, which makes a rattling sound. At the Sed festival that renewed his power, the king would engage in ritual dancing and shaking for Hathor. This festival, like Tekh, included aspects of drinking as well as music and dance.

❊

Hathor is one of the oldest Gods of Egypt, with roots in prehistoric cow-worshipping fertility cults. In myths from the dynastic periods, she took the form of a cow when she birthed the Sun God who was also her father, lifting him out of the waters of Nun. She was also his ferocious protector as the Eye of Ra in her form as Sekhmet. Shown as a woman wearing cow's horns with a solar disk, Hathor is at once the daughter of the Sun, the lover who welcomes him at the Western horizon with open arms and the mother who shelters him in her body overnight to rebirth him in the morning. Her name means "the house of Horus," a term also reserved in the Pyramid Texts for the part of the sky where the rejuvenation of the dead king took place. This is fitting for Hathor, as she assists the birthing of women and allows the rebirth of the dead.

Hathor was associated with kingship from the earliest period. As a mothering Goddess, she has a maternal relationship with all the child Gods of Egypt and with the kings. Horus is her son and the first king of Egypt, so all kings are Horus and they are all sons of Hathor, who sometimes appears as a cow suckling the kings.

Mothers are of course lovers first and Hathor has a distinctly erotic aspect throughout her myths of all eras, which contributed to her later association with Venus. Baskets of wooden phalluses—presumably votive offerings—were unearthed in early excavations of her shrine in the temple of Thutmose III. She was also patroness of erotic poetry. Hathor was associated in earlier periods with the night sky and with Venus as the evening star.

THE KHOIAK FESTIVALS

This series of interrelated festivals revolve around the life, death and rebirth of Osiris. This God was always depicted as a mummy, sometimes holding a crook and flail—the twin powers of civilization, herding and threshing—and sometimes with a green face to show his rotting body fertilizing the Nile and the land.

✳

Geb the Earth was the divine ruler of the land, naturally, but even his claim to the throne of Egypt was challenged. When he tried to don the crown of his father Shu—the air and sunlight first child of the creator—he was attacked by a vicious snake and had to prove his power against it and the enemies of Egypt. When his own son Wsjr (Osiris) inherited the kingdom he became the first king, the great king, the eternal king. At first he ruled in peace and prosperity, but then he, too, was challenged.

His brother Seth rose against him and who can know the cause? Many have said jealousy—either of power or of Isis—but there is no record of that time and the hearts of the Gods are hidden to humankind. Seth transformed himself into an animal—perhaps a bull, perhaps a crocodile—and on the night of a great storm, he killed his brother in some forlorn place where no one could see.

Osiris may have been trampled or he may have been drowned, or perhaps, being a God, he may have had to be killed in many ways. Another story tells that he died by trickery when Seth fashioned a golden chest just to fit Osiris and offered the beautiful treasure at a banquet to anyone who could fit into it. Many tried it for a jest, but none fit into it, for it was made to a brother's precise measurements. When Osiris tried it, the trap snapped shut and Seth soldered it shut and threw it into the Nile.

The Gods of the Delta all cried out in their mourning and their lament reached the ears of Isis. She knew immediately that her husband had died and so she began to search for his body. His coffin had drifted all the way to the city of Byblos in Lebanon and there it grew into a magnificent tree. The king of the city ordered the tree cut down so it could be carved into a pillar for his palace. After long searching Isis found the coffin that was now a pillar and demanded that it be given over to her. She brought her murdered husband's coffin back to Egypt with her but was quickly found out by Seth, who had assumed his brother's throne. Not trusting his divine sister's magic, Seth took his brother's body and tore it into fourteen pieces and scattered them across the Black Land.

With Nephthys, Isis searched for and restored each piece of the fallen God's corpse. The Goddesses mourned Osiris and watched over his body as they brought it back together. One by one they found them, one by one they restored the Great King. His penis had been thrown in the Nile and eaten by fish, so this Isis had to replace with a golden replica. Isis bound the pieces of his body with linen, restoring him to life in the dressing of death. Being the great-granddaughter of the creator who made the world in sexual power all alone, Isis was fully capable of reviving her husband to conceive her son. In the form of a bird she fanned him with her wings, bringing the breath of life back into his body. She knew the moment when Horus was conceived—and she cried out in her triumph. Her call reached the ears of the rest of the Gods, who appeared and bowed down to him and acknowledged him as king even before his birth.

Horus grew great for ten months in her womb before Isis birthed him in the Delta, where she hid the child in the thick growth of papyrus on a floating island. Here he was suckled by Hathor and protected by many of the Gods. But just as his grandfather Geb was attacked by a snake, just as Isis had contrived for Ra to be struck with venom, so, too, with Horus. Cursed by Seth, the babe was bitten and poisoned. His mother was unable to save him and so she appealed to the Gods with her spells. She appealed to her mother Nut, to her father Geb and to the creator Sun God who expelled the poison from the child just as she had once expelled poison from him.

In his greed, Seth reigned for centuries, taking every opportunity to abuse the young Horus. The two fighters Horus and Seth were equal in strength and there are many tales of their competitions. They transformed into hippos to see who could hold their breath the longest under water. They held a race in stone boats, which Horus won by making a boat out of wood which he painted to look like stone so that it sailed when Seth's stone boat sank. In another tale, Horus hunted Seth down in a boat, attacking him with a harpoon. In another version, it is Isis who wields the harpoon, but then she spares Seth because of the love she still has for her brother.

Knowing that it was Horus' right to rule but that his uncle's strength was too great to overcome, eventually Isis advised her son on how to dupe Seth into giving away some of his strength. Through this trickery Horus impregnated Seth, who gave birth to the disk of the sun through his head. Thoth crowned Horus with this solar disk, a symbol of his power and right to rule. Horus the falcon had the Sun and the Moon for his eyes, but one was torn out by Seth and had to be restored by Thoth.

The whole Earth and the Heavens and the Underworld were all being divided by the contention between the two Gods, so the rest of the Gods formed a tribunal headed by Geb to settle the matter. When they gathered at Heliopolis, Seth faced Horus once more. The tribunal had serious considerations to weigh. Seth was the most powerful of the Gods and they needed him to fight with Ra in his nightly battle against Apophis. And yet Horus was the legitimate heir to the throne of Egypt. Osiris supported his son from the Underworld by recalling to the other Gods that it was within his power to withhold crops from the Earth and that he could starve them all. In the end, the tribunal decided to divide the land between the Two Lords, giving Seth the South and Horus the fertile North, or giving Seth the desert and Horus the Black Land.

In some tales, Horus was awarded all of Egypt and Seth was assigned to live with Ra in the sky and guard his Boat of Millions of Years as he travels through the Underworld each night. In the hymns of Osiris, Seth was driven out altogether or cut to pieces in the form of a hippopotamus at the hands of Horus. During his coronation, Horus performed the funeral rite of the Opening of the Mouth for his father and raised the Djed Pillar for him.

In other versions, it was Osiris who stood against Seth before the tribunal, his body laying before them with Isis and Nephthys speaking

Osiris enthroned

as his representatives. Seth was unable to rationalize his treatment of his brother and so Osiris was vindicated as One True of Voice, the righteous dead. Only then was Osiris able to become the ruler of the Underworld.

In all the twists and turns of all the variations of the tale, Osiris was never resurrected to live again as a king on Earth. In his grief for himself, Osiris appealed to Atum. That great God told him that what Osiris considered his great misfortune was actually a blessing of fate. The events of his reign, murder and rejuvenation showed that he was favored beyond all others—for Osiris rules the Underworld in peace whereas the kingdoms on Earth will always suffer in striving and warfare.

COMMEMORATING OSIRIS

Just as every king was Horus on Earth, every king became Osiris in the Underworld. When a king celebrated the festival of Khoiak, he was commemorating the death of the God, of his own forebears and of himself. The Khoiak festivals reenacted the mythic cycle of Osiris' kingship, death, resurrection and installation as God of the dead.

Geographically widespread, this festival both mirrored and commemorated the scattering of Osiris' body parts across Egypt. This cycle informed both funerary practices and Egyptian beliefs around death. Isis bound the parts of Osiris' body together by wrapping them in linen, so the bodies of the dead were wrapped in linen for mummification. In addition to other cult activities, new images were fashioned each year of Osiris the Ennead and the jackal God Wepwawet, along with sacred boats for their transport.

There were two main activities in the festival: the public reenactment of the story of Osiris, and the individual creation of a representation of Osiris. For the first part, the king arrived at the temple of Osiris at Abydos and the priests laid myrrh, wine and other offerings before the God, who was fashioned in gold, turquoise and lapis. The statue was moved to a new shrine and surrounded by silver, copper, gold and fragrant cedar. Then the God took to his boat, appearing before the waiting crowd. The Opener of the Ways, the jackal Wepwawet, lead the way, parting the crowd before him. With a backdrop of tombs, the attack by the betrayer Seth was retold to the screams, gasps and delight of the onlookers, and the lucky even got to play a role. The falcons clashed on the banks of Nedit and Osiris was defeated by the rebels. In the end, Horus—played by the king—triumphed over his father's killers, slaying Seth and his company and declaring his victory to end the scene. But Osiris was still dead and must be laid to rest. His funeral procession wound to the tomb of King Djer of the first dynasty, which was considered Osiris' actual burial place. The people mourned and wept for their king as his funeral was performed, including an invocation to Ra to reinvigorate the body of the slain God.

On the twelfth through twenty-first days of the month, individuals commemorated the death of Osiris by creating figures of dirt mixed with grain, which they fashioned to human shape. They then wrapped them in linen to complete the mummies and decorated them in various ways. Some had green faces or masks and others wore crowns or sported phalluses to show off the God's ability to father a son even in death. These were either buried after a year or used in the maker's funeral. One set of instructions dictates that a woman playing the role of Shentayit—a minor Goddess associated with Isis—soak seeds in water from a sacred lake. This was to be mixed with sand, pressed into a cloth-lined mold, then watered daily for nine days. It was then unmolded, bound with strips of papyrus, and left out in the sun to be renewed by the energy of Ra. The next day it was wrapped in linen and placed in a coffin. The figurine would be buried at the following year's festival.

Many of these figurines have been excavated and the Karnak temple complex even included miniature catacombs for them. In other areas and periods they were buried directly in the Earth. The sheer number of them suggests that this was something done by many individuals in the community rather than by one priest on behalf of the community.

Both aspects of the festival—the reenactment and the formation of Osiris idols—are easily carried out by modern worshippers. Read the tale of Osiris' life, death and rebirth as king of the Underworld over several nights, ideally in the presence of statues of the God. Then create a grain and soil figure, water it, wrap it and keep it on your altar for a year to bring prosperity to your house. Bury it before making another.

SOKAR

Predating the unification of Egypt, Sokar was an ancient funerary God later conflated with Osiris. During the Old Kingdom, the Sokar festival was already a much-anticipated annual affair at the capital of Memphis.

�֎

Sokar began as a six-day festival and by the New Kingdom consumed the rest of the month. By the 26th, Osiris was considered to be dead and was reborn five days later on the first day of the festival of Nehebkau. People planted crops during the festival of Sokar and this became part of the Khoiak festival. Plant bulbs or seeds to honor this tradition.

The following is excerpted from a hymn to Osiris-Sokar:

Hail, royal one, coming forth in the body!
Hail, hereditary son, chief of the ranks
of the gods!
Hail, lord of many existences!
Hail, thou whose substance is like gold
in the temples!
Hail, lord of the duration of life, giver of years!
Hail, lord living throughout eternity!
Hail, lord worthy of many hundreds of thousands
of praises!
Hail, brilliant one, both at thy rising
and thy setting!
Hail to him who maketh pleasant all that
which breatheth!
Behold the lord of great fear and trembling
Hail, lord of many divinities!
Hail, resplendent one-with the white crown, lord
of the royal crown!

—translated by James Teackle Dennis, 1910

RAISING THE DJED PILLAR

The Djed Pillar is stability, the inherent strength of Osiris'
immutable state. It is his backbone, symbolized by a pillar of
reeds and representing the power of rebirth and renewal. It held
up the sky and each year at Memphis, the king raised it anew to
recommence his own power.

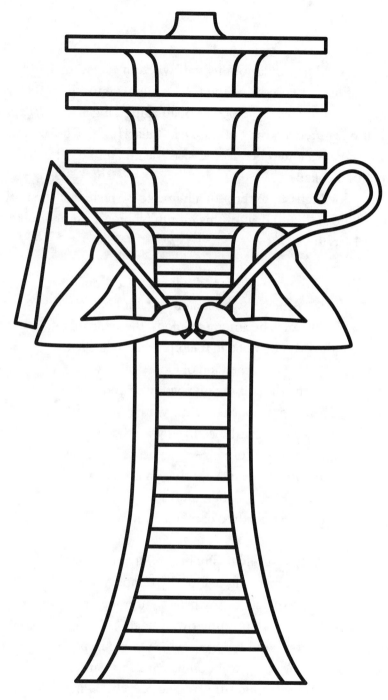

Djed Pillar

Ptah held the Djed Pillar on his staff where it joined the ankh, the symbol of life—two powers the God could give to kings. The Sed festival which renewed the power of an aging king after 30 years of reign also featured a raising of the Djed Pillar. In the Khoiak festival, it was a necessary step between Osiris' death and his rebirth at the feast of Nehebkau.

The following is an excerpt of a hymn to be recited at the festival on the 22nd and 26th days of this month by priestesses representing Isis and Nephthys:

> Lo! the two goddesses! Behold Osiris, bull of
> Amentit, who is alone established!
> Very great is he among the gods; the virile infant,
> the great heir of Sab [Geb,] born the image of
> the God of Gods!
> Come thou to the two widowed goddesses
> There goeth about thee the whole circle of the
> gods, and they meet with thee!
> Behold, Set cometh—grievous is his name
> when uttered near thy shrine, in presence of thy
> father, oh Ra—
> He is cast forth to contend with opponents
>
> Come surely to thy priests, striving and
> grieving before thy temple;
> Come surely to thy priests, in none other
> than thine own image!
> Our lord sitteth down in his temple in peace
> alone; the great conqueror is his name.
> After his long suffering he resteth, taking
> dangerous council against his enemies

He smiteth the land in his designs.
Go forth, great one with the gods;
And with thee the circle of the gods in front,
with the instrument-for-opening-the-mouth,
that it may equal thy perfection before
the gods.
Walk through the land entirely, great one
which art a body, with the royal Uraeus upon
his forehead.

−translated by James Teackle Dennis, 1910

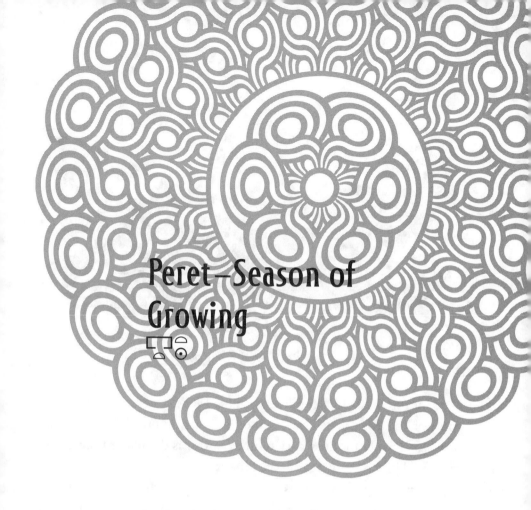

Peret–Season of Growing

Peret means growth, and this season encompasses the sowing and growing parts of the agricultural calendar. This season includes the months of Shefbedet, Rekehwer, Rekehnedjes and Renenutet, generally corresponding to the period from mid-November to mid-March:

Shefbedet   November 16–December 15
Rekehwer   December 16–January 14
Rekehnedjes   January 15–February 14
Renenutet   February 14th–March 15th

The scarab of Khepri

The month of Shefbedet opens with the Nehebkau festival, an extension of the Khoiak festival in the previous month. There are few festivals during this busy agricultural season, as the major festivals are clustered in the Flood season of Akhet.

The netjer of the season is Khepri, the God of the Sun at daybreak. His name comes from *kheper*, (to become,) and so Khepri is "one who is coming into being." Depicted as a scarab beetle, Khepri is a God of the Sun as well as rebirth and creation. The beetle rolls balls of dung like the Sun rolls across the sky. The scarab of Khepri appears in the *Book of Going Forth by Day* being placed over the heart of a person being mummified, to later be weighed against Ma'at in the Hall of Judgement.

Khepri had no temples, but scarab statues of him were both worn and set up in temple complexes. His mythology is one of rebirth and he is invoked in the *Book of Going Forth by Day* for this purpose. In the legend of the True Name of Ra, the Sun God Ra reveals that he is Khepri in the morning, Ra at noon and Atum in the evening, although sometimes this last is given as Amun. Khepri rode across the sky in the Day Boat and Atum sailed through the Underworld in the Night Boat. In the Underworld, the body parts of Khepri were separated and buried, and nevertheless arose anew in the morning. Thus he was invoked in funerary spells to prevent the putrefaction of the body. In the *Pyramid Texts*, he is named with Atum in the Hymn to the Sun in Utterance 587.

Hymn to the Sun
Greetings to thee, Atum.
Greetings to thee, Khepri, who created himself.

…

Thou comest into being, in thy
name of "Khepri."
Greetings to thee, eye of Horus, which he
adorned with his two hands completely.
He does not make thee hearken to the West;
he does not make thee hearken to the East;
he does not make thee hearken to the South;
he does not make thee hearken to the North;
he does not make thee hearken to those who are
in the middle of the land;
(but) thou harkenest to Horus.
It is he who adorned thee; it is he who built
thee; it is he who settled thee;
thou doest for him everything which he says
unto thee, in every place whither he goes.

–Samuel Mercer, 1952 (copyright not renewed)

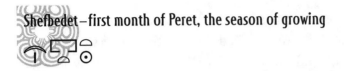 Shefbedet—first month of Peret, the season of growing

November 16–December 15

The significant festival during Shefbedet is Nehebkau, an extension of and closure to the Khoiak festivals. There is a lesser festival called Raising the Willow later in the month.

Make offerings this month to Khepri as the netjer of the season and to the virile God of fertility Min as the Netjer of the Month.

Significant dates:

1st of the month—November 16: Nehebkau
29th of the Month—December 14: Raising the Willow

THE FEAST OF NEHEBKAU, THE BEGINNING OF ETERNITY

Nehebkau is a serpent who is sometimes depicted with human legs or arms. He invests the *ka* (soul) in the body at the moment of birth, and then binds the ka to the *ba* (wandering soul) in death. The ka can be envisioned as a double of the person.

Snakes play a significant role as poisoners in Egyptian myth, and there are numerous spells against venom. Apophis is the ultimate example as the embodiment of chaos against whom Ra battles each night in the Duat. On the other hand, snakes are symbols of primordial power, particularly protective power as in the image of the uraeus, the rearing cobra found on crowns and other royal emblems. The body of Osiris is watched over by the *mehen* snake whose coils surround his corpse. In one tale, Ra sends his eye into the world in the form of a snake to find his children and she had power over all the other Gods.

The snake God Nehebkau was the son of a protective snake Goddess Renenutet, who watched over granaries and kitchens. She could be appealed to for sustenance and good harvest in life and for ongoing material providence in death.

This festival celebrates the resurrection of Osiris when his ka returns, a process which Nehebkau oversees. This happens five days after his death and as a celebration of renewal the festivities mirror the new year celebrations of the Wepet-renpet festival. To honor Osiris on this day, celebrate his resurrection and make offerings to Nehebkau and Renenutet to honor their role in his rebirth and to provide for you and yours. The following hymn to Osiris was translated by Wallis Budge in 1914.

[Praise be] unto thee,
O thou who extendest thine arms,
who liest asleep on thy side,
who liest on the sand,
the Lord of the earth,
the divine mummy...

Thou art the Child of the Earth Serpent,
of great age...

Ra-Khepera shineth upon thy body,
when thou liest on thy bed in the form of Seker,
so that he may drive away the darkness that
shroudeth thee,
and may infuse light in thy two eyes.

He passeth a long period of time shining upon
thee, and sheddeth tears over thee.

The earth resteth upon thy shoulders, and
its corners rest upon thee as far as the four pillars
of heaven.
If thou movest thyself, the earth quaketh.... [The
Nile] appeareth out of the sweat of thy two hands.
Thou breathest forth the air that is in thy throat
into the nostrils of men; divine is that thing
whereon they live.

Through thy nostrils subsist
the flowers,
the herbage,
the reeds,
the flags,
the barley,
the wheat,
and the plants whereon men live.

If canals are dug...
and houses and temples are built,
and great statues are dragged along,
and lands are ploughed up,
and tombs and funerary monuments are made,
they [all] rest upon thee.

It is thou who makest them.

They are upon thy back.
They are more than can be done into writing.

There is no vacant space on thy back, they all lie
on thy back, and yet [thou sayest] not,

"I am [over] weighted therewith.
Thou art the father and mother of
men and women,
they live by thy breath,
they eat the flesh of thy members.

Rekehwer—second month of Peret, the season of growing

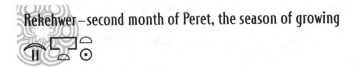

December 16–January 14

Offer to the netjer of the season, Khepri, and the netjer of the month, Rekhur.

The major festival comes at the end of the month: Amun in the Festival of Raising Heaven. Take note of the following date:

> *30th of the month—January 14*: Amun in the Festival of Raising Heaven

AMUN IN THE FESTIVAL OF RAISING HEAVEN

This festival spanned several days and began on the 30th of the month of Rekehwer. It is also called the day of bringing branches of the Ished tree, which was a tree of life. During this festival, the statue of the God went out from the temple to give oracles and visit other temples.

✳

Amun's name means "hidden," and he is the embodiment of the hidden force of creation in the world. Eminently mysterious, Amun's origins are shrouded. Originally an air God of a set of primordial Gods called the Ogdoad in Hermopolis, by the end of the Middle Kingdom, he was the most prominent among the Gods and his worship had been adopted in Thebes.

His original spouse was simply a feminized version of his name: Amaunet. However, by the Middle Kingdom, his spouse was Mut and Khonsu the potter—the creator who spun the world on his wheel—was his son. These three Gods made up the Theban Triad.

In the New Kingdom, Amun was combined with Ra to become Amun-Ra, the creator of the world, the king of Gods and the force of creation all at once.

Mut's name most likely means "mother" and she was frequently shown with Khonsu in her lap. However, she should not be treated as a mother Goddess in a reductionist manner—she wore the double crown of unified Egypt, representing the power of kingship. Rulers were called "child of Amun and Mut," so she granted great power and authority. Every royal birth was the result of the union of Mut and Amun and each king drank in his power from his mother Mut's milk.

Amun lacks the rich, detailed mythology of most Gods but he does have some stories. In one, he is a primeval goose, the Great Shrieker, who laid the world egg which he fertilized himself in serpent form. In the New Kingdom, he embodied virility as the God who generated all life and who was responsible for ongoing creation through his sexual potency.

Most Egyptian Gods have homes. They can reside in their temples, statues and many places at once but they do have particular locations. Amun, on the other hand, while he also had temples and statues, has a spirit and a presence that can be felt anywhere and was compared to the wind.

Although Egyptian religion was temple-based, it was still accessible to common people. The inner recesses of temples were reserved for priests in a state of purity, but other parts of temples were open to the people at least on certain occasions. In the Middle Kingdom, there were chapels of the ear, which were specifically for prayer so that the people could pray to the Gods. Located at the back of temples, these chapels could be entered without having to enter the temple itself. In some complexes, certain courtyards were reserved for ordinary people petitioning the Gods. Doorways to the outside were always accessible, even when the people could not go any further into the temple and thus they served as places of prayer. One of Amun's titles is Amun-Ra in the Thickness of the Door, referring to just this sort of portal.

The wealthy had the option of placing statues of themselves within the temple precinct so that they could always be with the Gods. These could also act as intercessors when called upon. Outside the temple, worshippers could contact the Gods through stelae engraved with ears—which could be carried or kept in the home—and through shrines that were not part of any temple complex. People could use these to offer votive figurines as well as for prayer.

All Egyptians could be contacted by the Gods in dreams and there were also, less commonly, *rekhet* or mediums in the broader community. These—all women—were able to contact the Gods and determine their role in a person's particular situation of concern. The Gods are generally kindly, but their displeasure could manifest in the form of various misfortunes. These could be revealed by oracles at festivals and in processions, but when these were unavailable a rekhet could establish whether a God had placed a spell on a person, and if so, how to lift it and regain the favor of the God.

"He speaketh the gentle word at the
moment of strife.
He is a pleasant breeze to him that
appealeth to him.
He delivereth the helpless one.
He is the wise god whose plans are beneficent…
He is more helpful than millions to the man
who hath set him in his heart."

–from a hymn to Amun, tr. Wallis Budge, 1914

Rekehnedjes—third month of Peret, the season of growing

January 15—February 14

This month's festival of Ptah falls at the beginning of the month. Festivals with this name appear on various days in various places. This date may be a local Theban festival. Ptah is nonetheless a prominent deity throughout Egypt and should be celebrated in the calendar year. On the same day, the statue of Amun that had gone out from the temple during Amun in the Festival of Raising Heaven was returned to its naos. Make offerings to Khepri as the netjer of the season, and to Amun-Ra as the netjer of the month.

Take note of this significant date:

1st of the month—January 15th: Festival of Ptah
1st of the month—January 15th: Return of the statue of Amun

FESTIVAL OF PTAH

In the primordial waters of Nun, Ptah formed Atum with his heart and his tongue. He had created himself already and went on to make the whole world in the same way, with his thought and his word. The most prominent God in the capital of Memphis, he is Ptah the creator, Ptah the architect who framed the universe. He is usually depicted as a man wrapped in a cloak wearing a false beard, or as a mummy. His head bears the skullcap of the artisan. He holds a staff that has both the ankh—the symbol of life—and the Djed Pillar, the spine of Osiris that holds up the heavens. This scepter of Ptah was a symbol of ultimate authority, which he bestowed on rulers when they were coronated in his temple.

The Apis bull is the ba or soul of Ptah, and it had its own enclosure in many of Ptah's temples. His spouse was the fierce lioness Sekhmet, and

Ptah the creator

they had a son, the lotus God Nefertem. Imhotep is another child of Ptah and this son is both human and historical. Deified after his death, Imhotep was the architect who designed the first pyramid, Djoser's step pyramid.

Called Lord of Ma'at, Benevolent of Face and Great of Strength, Ptah could be petitioned to aid Egypt in times of trouble, and in one famous example, he raised an army of rats to drive out the attacking Assyrians from the town of Pelusium. The vermin gnawed at their shield straps, their quivers and even their bowstrings until the invaders retreated and left the city in peace.

Inventor of all the arts and a patron of craftsmen, Ptah himself could even craft a new body for a person who was deceased. He is the author of the Opening of the Mouth, a ceremony used in funerary rites which reinvests the ka soul in statues and mummified corpses.

"I have opened thy mouth.
I have opened thy two eyes.
I have opened thy mouth with the
instrument of Anpu.
I have opened thy mouth with the Meskha
instrument wherewith the mouth of the gods
was opened.
Horus openeth the mouth and
eyes of the Osiris.
Horus openeth the mouth of the Osiris even as he
opened the mouth of his father.

As he opened the mouth of the god Osiris so shall
he open the mouth of my father with the iron
that cometh forth from Set, with the Meskha
instrument of iron wherewith he opened the
mouth of the gods shall the mouth of the Osiris
be opened.

And the Osiris shall walk and shall talk, and his
body shall be with the Great Company of the
Gods who dwell in the Great House of the Aged
One (i.e. the Sun-god) who dwelleth in Anu.

And he shall take possession of the Urrt Crown
therein before Horus, the Lord of mankind.

Hail, Osiris!"

−excerpt from the *Opening of the Mouth, Pyramid
Texts*, tr. by Wallis Budge, 1914

Renenutet—fourth month of Peret, the season of growing

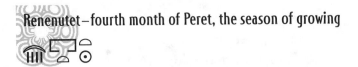

February 14th–March 15th

Offer to Khepri as the netjer of the season, and to Renenutet as the netjer of the month.

The major festival of the month is the Festival of Bast, also called the Day of Chewing Onions for Bast. Later in the month, you can see the transition to the harvest season beginning with two offerings to Renenutet. Her festival falls on the first day of the next month, which is also the first day of the harvest season Shemu and the birthday of her son Nepri, the God of grain or grain personified. These offerings were important preliminary steps before the harvest celebrations began.

Take note of these dates:

4th of the month—*February 17*: Day of Chewing Onions for Bast
25th of the month—*March 10*: Harvest Offering to Renenutet
27th of the month—*March 12*: Granary Offering to Renenutet

DAY OF CHEWING ONIONS FOR BAST

Throngs of festival-goers crowded boats headed for Bubastis, and made music the whole journey. When each step and each splash of oars was accompanied by flute and sistrum, how could there be anything unpleasant, anything but bliss in the celebration of the gracious Goddess of pleasure? How sweet her hospitality must have felt when they reached the island of her temple and took to the shade of the sacred grove! How intense the joy of the feast, at which more wine was drunk than in the whole rest of the year! When the day of procession came and the parade wound its bawdy way through the city, a cacophony of music and laughter filled the air, competing with the smell of wine and incense.

Herodotus is a late, foreign and unreliable source, but he gives an intriguing description of the festival of Bast held at Bubastis each year. Women were released from obligations to propriety and celebrated by singing, dancing, drinking and showing their genitalia. He claims that over seven hundred thousand worshippers attended the festival, likely an exaggerated number. Nonetheless, the festival was renowned for its popularity throughout Egypt.

One of the cult activities of the festival was the presentation to the temple of mummified cats to offer to the Goddess. Bast protected Egypt and the people of Egypt just as a cat protects a house from vermin. Perhaps this is why amulets with images of Bast were given on the New Year, to drive out any lingering bad luck from the five intercalary days.

The onion title is likely due its position in the calendar. As in other places, onions are an early harvest crop in Egypt. Additionally, they grow beneath the ground, giving them a touch of the underworld. The agricultural cycle begins with Sokar–Osiris and early sowing in the Khoiak festival, so pulling up onions from beneath the Earth and consuming them for or offering them to a protective Goddess completes this cycle without any lingering funerary miasma.

Bast

Attested since the Old Kingdom, Bast originated in Bubastis but her cult spread across Egypt. In various times and places, Bast was associated with Hathor, Mut, Tefnut and Isis. Her most enduring association was in Memphis with Sekhmet, where the Goddesses became simultaneous, contrasting forms of one another. Bast the daughter of Ra was the kinder aspect of the Eye of Ra where Sekhmet was the fierce aspect. Sekhmet ruled war and plague where Bast ruled sex and fertility and protected women and babies.

The Goddess Bast

These lines between the two Goddesses were not always neat. Bast shows up in spells to both cause and ward off sickness. Like Sekhmet, she was a mother to kings and served as their protector. Mothers fiercely avenge wrongs against their children and Bast could be a ferocious guardian. In the Predynastic and Old Kingdom periods, she was sometimes a lion, but by the Middle Kingdom, Bast was most always represented as a woman with the head of a cat or as a sleek, black cat.

In one tale, a prince called Setna happens upon Taboubu, a daughter of a priest of Bast. He is immediately infatuated with her and will do anything to have her. Setna arranges to meet Taboubu in Bast's temple in Memphis, but when he arrives, she refuses to sleep with him until some conditions are met. First he signs over all his worldly goods to her. Then he arranges for his children to sign over their claims to them. But even that is not enough. Like a cat toying with a mouse, the beautiful Taboubu—now clad in the thinnest and most revealing linen—demands that Setna allow her to kill his children! Anything for the bewitching daughter of the priest. He agrees and they are slain. When at last she reaches out to him, smiling seductively, Setna takes off his clothes and moves toward her, leading her to the bed. In the very moment when he takes her, she vanishes and the prince finds himself in the middle of a road in public, naked and having a very intimate encounter with a clay vessel. Taboubu had been an illusion—or perhaps even the Goddess herself in disguise—tricking the wicked prince in retribution. He had stolen a book from a tomb and the Goddess punishes those who offend the laws of heaven.

HARVEST AND GRANARY OFFERINGS TO RENENUTET

The name Renenutet means "the nourishing snake," and this cobra Goddess is associated with sustenance, luck and fertility. Sometimes she is depicted as a snake, sometimes as a woman with a snake's head. Associated with maternity and particularly with mother's milk, she is also sometimes shown suckling a baby. The nourishing and healing qualities of both food and milk fall under Renenutet's domain and as the mother of the grain God, she had significant influence over the harvest as well.

As Lady of the Granaries Renenutet chased mice and other vermin from granaries and food storage areas, protecting the sustenance of the family as well as the broader community.

As a snake she can be seen on the uraeus, the protective cobra on the crown of kings. Nonetheless, Renenutet the Mistress of Provisions was unfailingly gracious and was frequently revered in the home. Many Egyptian households had small cobra-shaped bowls that might have served as offering places to her or representations of her.

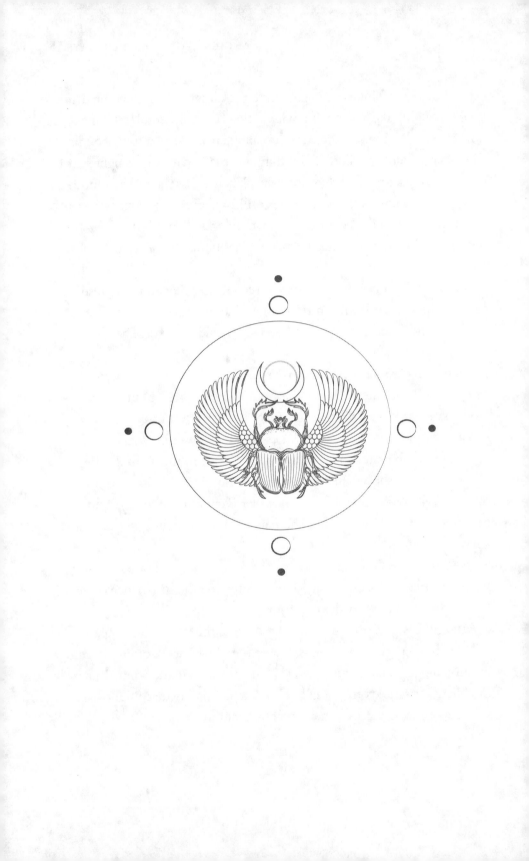

Shemu – Harvest Season of Low Water

S hemu means "low water" and was the harvest season that followed the growing period of Peret. The shining fields yielded up emmer and einkorn wheat as well as lentils and barley. These staple crops made up the bulk of the Egyptian diet (and food offerings to the Gods,) along with onions, garlic, lettuces and fruits.

This season includes the following months:

Khonsu	March 16–April 14
Khentkhety	April 15–May 14
Ipet-Hemet	May 15–June 13
Wepet-renpet	June 14–July 13

The sound of Shemu in ancient Egypt is one familiar to so many other forms of repetitive labor across the world—music. Ancient Egyptian farmers harvesting the fields sang work songs to keep the rhythm of reaping and help endure hard labor in the hot Sun. In other aspects of Egyptian life, music included percussion such as drums and rattles, woodwind flutes and stringed harp and lyre-like instruments. In the fields, though, music mostly took the form of call and response songs, although some images show flutes accompanying the workers. Some songs tell folk tales and myths and others take the form of bragging about how hard the singers are working. One song recorded in the tomb of Paheri, a nomarch or regional governor in Upper Egypt, entreats the worker by praising the weather, describing how nice it is to work the fields on a breezy day.

This is a good day!
To the land come out!
The North Wind is out.
The sky works according to our heart!
Let us work, binding firm our heart.

Paheri's tomb also includes a song for the oxen who worked the threshing floor:

Thresh for yourselves. Thresh for yourselves.
Thresh for yourselves. Thresh for yourselves.
Straw to eat, corn for your masters.
Let not your hearts be weary, your lord
is pleased.

–tr. Francis Llewellyn Griffith, 1917

In addition to the festivals, this season is followed by the five Epagomenal days from July 14th–18th. These intercalary days fall between the old year and the new. The Sky Goddess Nut lay with her brother Geb—the Earth—and conceived children. However, Ra—ever the defender of order—did not desire any new powers to upset the balance of the world. To prevent Nut from birthing these new Gods, he declared that she could give birth on no day in the year. And so Nut suffered, heavy in pregnancy with five children, until she and Thoth gambled the Moon for enough light to create five days, one for each birth. Each intercalary day is for the birth of a God brought forth by Nut after she evaded her curse, so they are the birthdays of Osiris, Horus, Seth, Isis and Nephthys. In accordance with the word of Ra, however, they are on no day of the year and so they are dangerous and unlucky days.

The netjer of the low water season is Khonsu-Ra. Khonsu is the Moon God of the cycles of time and in this form, he is conflated with Ra and represents an aspect of the creator God.

Khonsu—first month of Shemu, the harvest season of low water

March 16th–April 14th

The beginning of the harvest season in ancient Egypt aligns nicely with the arrival of the first Spring crops in the rest of the northern hemisphere. Make offerings to Khonsu-Ra as netjer of the season and Khonsu as the netjer of the month.

Take note of the following significant dates:

First of the month—March 16: Festival of Renenutet and birth of Nepri, the personification of grain
10th of the month—March 25: Adoration of Anubis
New Moon in this month:—Festival of Min

The procession of Min was a lunar holiday, and so the precise date varies. It was celebrated on the New Moon of this month. For exact dates for upcoming years, see the table of New Moon festival dates in the Appendices.

Khonsu, meaning "the traveller," was the ancient Egyptian name for the God of the Moon, the shifting, restless God of Time. He was associated with Thoth, another deity who marked the passing of time. In an echo of his pull on the tides, Khonsu controlled the rising and falling fertility of crops, animals and humans and was called Khonsu the Provider. Khonsu loved to play games, especially the board game *senet*.

Khonsu was also called Lord of Ma'at in Thebes, where his image very much resembles that of Ptah. A vigorous bull at the New Moon and a neutered bull at the Full Moon, he represents renewal and the cycles of renewal. He was depicted as a mummy bearing the forelock of young men and the beard of mature men, kings and Gods. He sometimes holds a crook and flail and his head bears the Moon in both full and crescent forms and he wears a necklace with a crescent Moon and keyhole. He was occasionally shown with the head of a falcon.

He formed a member of holy triads in both parts of the country—in the North Khonsu was the son of Ptah and Sekhmet, in the South a child of Amun and Mut. He was renowned for his great power to heal and drive out demons. A stele from the reign of Ramses II tells a tale of how the king lent a statue of Khonsu to a king of Bactria to help heal his daughter. After Khonsu-the-Plan-Maker had driven out the spirits of disease from the princess, the king delayed returning the statue because he was so impressed with the God's power. He had a dream of a golden falcon leaving the shrine and flying away back to Egypt and decided to return the statue after all.

The Moon and its God can be shifting and tricky, and at times even vicious. In the Coffin Texts, Khonsu is called "the one who lives on hearts" and he appears in the Cannibal Hymn of the Pyramid as teaching kings to devour the hearts of the other Gods, a practice he indulges in himself. But is time not a devourer of all things, even of the Gods?

FESTIVAL OF RENENUTET AND BIRTHDAY OF NEPRI

Nepri was the personification of the harvest grain and was strongly associated with Osiris. On the day of her son's birth, honor Renenutet the mother. She is not only the mother who protects but also the perfect mother, in which form she is merged with Isis. She can be called "She Who Rears Up" to honor the protective aspect of her motherhood, as she was the snake who protected children from bad luck and curses. She also gave babies their secret names in their mother's milk, as she was associated with nursing. Names were considered to have immense power and a person's name and image must survive for them to have an afterlife. As a name-giver, Renenutet is associated with fate itself.

Anubis

ADORATION OF ANUBIS

The adoration of Anubis was a minor and likely regional festival. The God himself, though, is prominent in funerary beliefs as well as art and literature related to death. He was called "First of the Westerners," the West being the land of the dead because the Sun dies in the West. By the Middle Kingdom, this title had largely transferred to Osiris. Anubis is also called, "The Dog Who Swallows Millions," "Master of Secrets" and "The Lord of the Sacred Land."

His name is similar to both the Egyptian words for "rot" and "puppy." The ancient jackal-headed psychopomp is frequently identified with the even older jackal God Wepwawet. Anubis appears in the artwork of First Dynasty tombs, but he is likely older. Given the Egyptian fear of dismemberment and putrefaction of the body, it is probable that he originated as a deity intended to ward off wild dogs who might be inclined to disturb fresh corpses. His skin in both jackal and jackal-headed human form is black, representing rot and by extension the fertile black soil of the Nile valley, just as Osiris has a green face to represent the fertility that comes from the decay of his body. Anubis could also be represented by an animal skin attached to a stick or pole—the *imy-wt*.

Anubis tended corpses as well as protected them and he is frequently shown in scenes of mummification. His priests were responsible for mummifying the deceased and they wore masks of Anubis when performing that sacred rite. In the myths of Osiris, Anubis both invents mummification and personally tends and protects the body of the God. By the Middle Kingdom, Anubis was considered a son of Osiris and Nephthys, although earlier he was thought to be a child of Ra and Hesat the cow Goddess or sometimes Bast.

Anubis plays a key role in the afterlife, escorting souls to the Hall of Truth to be judged and assisting with the weighing of the deceased's heart against the feather of Ma'at. He also punishes those who rob tombs or enter them forcibly, and images of him are frequently found guarding over the entrances to tombs. He did this with great ferocity. In one tale, Seth attempts to approach the body of Osiris while Anubis was guarding it. He had disguised himself as a leopard, but Anubis recognized him nonetheless and took a hot iron and branded Seth with it all over his body. This is why—the story goes—leopards have spots. But Anubis was not yet satisfied with his punishment of the evildoer. He skinned Seth and wore his hide around his shoulders so that all whose gaze fell upon him would be warned against disturbing the dead.

PROCESSION OF MIN

Before the phallic God came forth from his temple, the games in his honor had already begun. Men competed to show off their strength and virility by raising and then climbing a massive pole for the festival pavilion. When he finally came out, carried by his priests, he was accompanied by singers and dancers as he travelled through the fields to bless them with fruitfulness.

When the God's boat came to the king, it stopped. The king himself—in the presence of the most fecund of Gods—cut the first grain of the harvest to sustain the life of his people. He offered it to the black-skinned God in the presence of the people. The God is black as the soil is black and his fertile power is its power and the king's power as well.

Older than Egypt, Min was honored in the predynastic period and always depicted with an erect penis. A God of sexuality and fertility, it is through his potency that the land gives life, and he is able to bless people and animals as well as crops. He is also frequently shown with lettuce plants, which were one of his favorite offerings. Lettuce in ancient Egypt is a tall plant that can excrete a milky white liquid.

His earliest representations were all vaguely phallic: door bolts, lightning bolts, barbed arrows, fossilized fish. In dynastic times, sometimes Min was shown as the constellation Orion, with the three prominent stars of his belt forming the phallus of the God. He frequently holds the flail typically seen with Osiris and Ptah—and occasionally he holds both his penis and the flail . He has strong associations with Osiris, Set, Amun, Horus, Ptah and the Moon. By far his most enduring link, though, is with the kings, or rather with the power of kingship itself. A king who could not ensure the fertility of the land was not king for long. Without strength, particularly in the form of sexual vigor, a king was unfit to rule. For this reason, kings had to prove themselves at their heb-sed festivals that renewed their power after 30 years of reign. Min was also involved in those festivals.

To honor this holiday, carry a statue of Min through your fields or garden. You can also create a phallic representation and draw his name in hieroglyphs on it and use that in the same manner. Offer your first fruits to him and the presence of the God will bring abundance.

Khentkhety—second month of Shemu, the harvest season of low water

April 15th–May 14th

The New Moon of this month is the date of the Wadi feast—the Beautiful Feast of the Valley. See the Appendix for a table of these dates. Make offerings to Heru—Horus—as the netjer of the months and Khonsu-Ra as the netjer of the season.

Hymn to the Sun
Well dost thou watch, O Horus,
who sailest over the sky,
thou child who proceedest from
the divine father,
thou child of fire,
who shinest like crystal, who destroyest
the darkness and the night.

Thou child who growest rapidly, with gracious
form, who restest in thine eye.
Thou wakest up men who are asleep on their
beds, and the reptiles in their nests.
Thy boat saileth on the fiery Lake Neserser, and
thou traversest the upper sky by means
of the winds thereof.
The two daughters of the Nile-god crush for
thee the fiend Neka, Nubti (i.e. Set)

...

Thine enemy hath fallen, and Truth standeth
firm before thee.
When thou again transformest thyself
into Tem,
thou givest thy hand to the Lords of Akert
(i.e. the dead),
those who lie in death give thanks for thy
beauties when thy light falleth upon them.
They declare unto thee what is their hearts'
wish, which is that they may see thee again.
When thou hast passed them by, the darkness
covereth them, each one in his coffin.
Thou art the lord of those who cry out to thee,
the god who is beneficent for ever.
Thou art the Judge of words and deeds, the
Chief of chief judges, who stablishest truth, and
doest away sin.

−translated by Wallis Budge, 1914

NEW MOON: WADI, THE BEAUTIFUL FEAST OF THE VALLEY

The priests and the people purified themselves on the east bank of the river. The statues of Amun, Mut and Khonsu were carried out from their sanctuaries and journeyed across the Nile in a golden boat from Karnak to Thebes—from the land of the living to the land of the dead. The cliffs on the west bank contained a necropolis and were themselves seen as the edge of the Underworld, a gateway over which Hathor stood guard. Priests lucky enough to be assigned this most sacred duty stood guard on top of the cliffs as well.

Once the decorated *Usherhat* barge had landed, priests led the statues out, waving fans before them to signal the presence of the divine. Throngs of people clad in white linen and adorned with *weseh* collars made of flowers met the procession with food offerings and followed it as the statues of dead kings and Gods were paraded through the roads of tombs.

Women, men, children and grandparents all followed, trying to catch a glimpse as Amun went visiting through the royal tombs and temples, including that of the current king. It was this moment—when the God rests in the temple of the living king—that the king becomes divine again and his power is renewed. He is made eternal and the kings before him are once again revived through the same process. Life, death and eternity all converge at Thebes.

The clatter of the sistrum and the *menat* necklace could be heard throughout the graveyards. On this first day of the two-day festival, noise-making was essential. The cacophony revived the spirits dwelling within the necropolis, entreating them to come out of their tombs and visit their families. At this time the people held feasts at family sepulchers—called "houses of the heart's joy"—to make offerings of food and flowers to their dead and celebrate with drinking, dancing and song. Statues of the dead would be taken out of their crypts and physically placed among their living family members to take part in the feast. Hathor the Lady of Drunkenness presided and wine and beer helped the living enter into an ecstatic union with the dead. The Beautiful Feast of the Valley promised rebirth and regeneration to the personal as well as royal dead, and to the ordinary citizen as well as to the king.

The feasting in the necropolis continued through the night, the rhythm of percussion and hymns sung to ancestors continuing to rise and fall even as the sun fell below the horizon. The smells of meat, wine and sweet myrrh oil filled the place so that surely the spirits of the dead would be drawn out to partake in the celebration.

The statue of the God spent the night before the cliffs—before the Duat—in union with Hathor and thus the world was renewed. This sexual merging of the divine, of the celestial in the place of the dead, was so potent that the temple where this occurred became a site of pilgrimage for those seeking fertility charms.

This Theban celebration originated in the Middle Kingdom and continued to be celebrated through the New Kingdom. Appropriately for a holiday of ancestry, the Wadi feast still echoes through Egyptian cultural practices. Modern monotheistic Egyptians of all creeds still visit the graves of their dead to eat and drink with them, so the custom survives even if the particulars of timing and ritual have changed. To celebrate this holiday, have a picnic on the grass at the graves of your own beloved dead. If none are buried near you, bring their pictures or mementos to a nearby graveyard and make offerings to both the local deceased and your own loved ones. Remember always to include Hathor, the Lady of Heaven, the Lady of Drunkenness.

Ipet-Hemet—third month of Shemu, the harvest season of low water

May 15th–June 13th

The days grow longer and hotter and the water level in the river drops noticeably. The significant festival for this summer month is Neith. The netjer of the season is Khonsu-Ra and the netjer of the month is Wadjet. Take note of the following dates:

> *13th of the month—May 27*: Neith, the Festival of the Lamps
> *15th of the month—May 29*: offerings to Hapi and Amun to secure a good flood

WADJET

An ancient Goddess of protection, Wadjet can be seen on the white crown as the uraeus, the rearing cobra. She is particularly associated with the protection of Lower Egypt and with her sister Nekhbet the vulture Goddess, the protector of Upper Egypt. Together they were the Two Ladies who protected the king and at his coronation each king was given the title "He of the Two Ladies." They work together for the protection of both the king and the nation, in contrast to the Two Lords of Egypt—Horus and Seth, who also represent the northern and southern parts of the country. While these two are in constant conflict, the Two Ladies cooperate to support and defend the unified kingdom.

As a daughter of Ra, Wadjet shows up in stories about the Eye of Ra, the fierce protector Goddess associated with Sekhmet and Hathor. Wadjet is typically depicted as a cobra but also sometimes appears as lion-headed woman, echoing her connection to Sekhmet and the Eye Goddesses. The Two Ladies are most frequently shown together with the cobra of Wadjet on the king's crown while Nekhbet hovers overhead. They also appear as women standing on either side of the king.

Wadjet's body formed the first papyrus plant and she is called *Weret-Hekau*, "Great of Magic." She protected the common people just as she guarded the kings and can be petitioned to aid against ghosts, ill luck and evil spirits.

NEITH AND THE FESTIVAL OF LAMPS

Her name likely means, "The Terrifying One," but she is called, "Mother of the Gods," "Mother of the Father of All Things," and "The Great Goddess." Neith's veneration in Egypt lasted thousands of years—from the Predynastic period to the conquest by Rome. A mother Goddess, she invented birth so that she could bring forth the creator. She also presided over war and creation and wove the shrouds for mummification of the dead.

It was at her command that the waters of Nun began to shift and move so that the benben mound could rise out of them. Sometimes Neith is considered to be the primordial water itself, giving rise to her fertility associations. She gave birth to Ra and also formed the chaos-snake Apophis from her spit, not to foil Ra but to balance him, upholding Ma'at. She also represents balance when she is depicted as a wife of Set, as she upholds justice in the tales of Horus and Set, rightfully conferring the rulership of Egypt on Horus.

Some depictions of Neith show a woman with a phallus, again emphasizing balance. She could also be depicted sitting on a throne with two arrows crossing a shield in her warlike aspect. She appears with implements of weaving in her funerary role or wearing the red crown in her mother aspect. She is shown as a woman with the head of a crocodile, suckling baby crocodiles when she is the primordial water.

Her primary center of worship was her city of Sais and she was more prominent in lower Egypt than upper. She was honored throughout the country, however, and was a powerful intermediary between heaven and the realm of mankind.

To bring Earth into balance with Heaven, Neith oversaw the land mirroring the sky in her Festival of the Lamps. People gathered from all over Egypt and when night fell the crowds lit candles and lamps to appear from above as the stars in the sky appear from below. The festival was focused in Sais, but Egyptians across the land lit lamps in Neith's honor on this night. The lights attracted the dead and lit the pathways for them to visit the living, just as the stars illuminated the paths to the Gods. Light your own lamp on this night to uphold balance and honor the Goddess.

Wepet-renpet – fourth month of Shemu, the harvest season of low water

June 14th–July 13th

The days are long and hot and the fields are beginning to dry out, threatening to return to desert in this last month before the flood and the new year. The netjer of the season is Khonsu-Ra and the netjer of the month is Heru-Khuiti. The major festival of the month is for Isis. Take note of the date:

2nd of the month—June 15: Festival of Isis

Heru-Khuiti—Horus of the Horizon—is typically anglicized to Horakhty. He is frequently conflated with Ra in this form to be Ra-Her-Khuiti—or Ra-Horakhty—as "Ra who is Horus of the Horizon." Heru-Khuiti is the God of the Sun as it sets and rises. He was depicted as the solar falcon or as man with a falcon's head bearing the solar disk and/or a crown with the uraeus. Honor the God representing the Sun in its greatest power in this last month of summer.

FESTIVAL OF ISIS

There is little surviving information about the details of this late period festival of Isis. Roman sources describe festivals for her outside of Egypt, which involved processions in which priests with shaved heads carried garlands of flowers. Of her festivals in Egypt, however, little is known. Herodotus—another foreign source—tells of a festival for Isis in which there was sacrifice followed by lamentation by all present. That could reflect this festival or a different one.

Winged Isis

A child of Nut and Geb—Earth and Sky—Isis was the sister and wife of Osiris and the mother of Horus. She was the throne, the seat of power, and the hieroglyph of a throne even formed part of her name. By extension, she was the mother not only of Horus but of every Egyptian king. Called Weret-Hekau, "Great of Magic," like Wadjet, she is sometimes shown as a cobra who suckles the kings of Egypt.

Isis is primarily depicted as a woman with a throne headdress, and is also associated with the kite falcon, a knot and the sistrum. In one tale from the *Contendings of Horus and Seth*, Isis runs Seth through with a harpoon, but then spares his life when he appeals to her as his sister. This so angered Horus that he cut his mother's head off. Thoth replaced it with a cow's head, so she also appears as a woman with the head of a cow. Herodotus relates that while bulls were sacrificed to the Gods in Egypt, cows could not be slaughtered because they were sacred to Isis.

Her popularity increased over time and by the Ptolemaic era, her domain included magic, agriculture and all crafts and institutions. She taught the arts of spinning, weaving and grinding grain. Isis was identified with Sirius, the star that foretold the inundation. She was eventually worshipped outside of Egypt and her cult became popular throughout the Roman empire. It is a late Latin source—Apuleius—who calls Isis the Great Goddess and claims that all other Goddesses are merely names and faces of her. Although there is no indication that this belief was an aspect of her Egyptian worship (and likely reflects the rising influence of monotheism and mystery cults during the author's time,) it does reflect the broad appeal that she had because her character is eminently powerful, magnanimous and gracious.

Best known for gathering and reviving the body of Osiris to conceive Horus, many stories of Isis revolve around protecting and providing for the baby Horus while hiding him in the marsh and tricking and hunting Seth. In *Isis and the True Name of Ra*, she is more clever than all the other Gods and learns the true names of every single thing on Earth and in heaven. The only name Isis doesn't know—and therefore doesn't have power over—is the name of her father Ra. She decides to challenge him for this power when he begins to show the creeping signs of old age. When he begins to drool, she knows he is weak and she acts. Knowing that only the greatest power could harm Ra even in his lessened state, she uses his own power against him.

When the saliva slips unwittingly from his mouth, Isis gathers up a little bit from where it lands in the dirt. Mixing it with more dirt, Isis fashions Ra's spit into a snake and hides it at a cross-roads where she knows that Ra will pass by. The next morning, Ra walks by this place and is bitten by the snake. His scream is so fierce, so loud, so horrible that even the Gods are disturbed by the sound. The venom begins to spread through his body: simultaneously hot and cold, Ra is dripping with sweat and loses his vision. His arms and legs shake and his lips tremble as he announces that he has been harmed by a creature that he did not himself create.

Ra summons all the Gods to his side to see who can come to his aid. Feigning ignorance, Isis promises to curse the attacker with magic. The she tells Ra that she can help him with her magic if only he will tell her his true name. He agrees and regales her with a list of his titles and accomplishments and then reveals that he is Khepri in the morning, Ra at noon and Atum in the evening. But these are not his true names. Isis offers again to help, saying that she can only do so if she knows his true name.

Eventually the God's suffering becomes so great that he calls his daughter Isis to him and leaning close, whispers his true name in her ear and tells her to pass the name to Horus when he will be born, though he is not yet conceived. She then uses her magic to draw out the poison, but one day her own child will suffer snakebite as well.

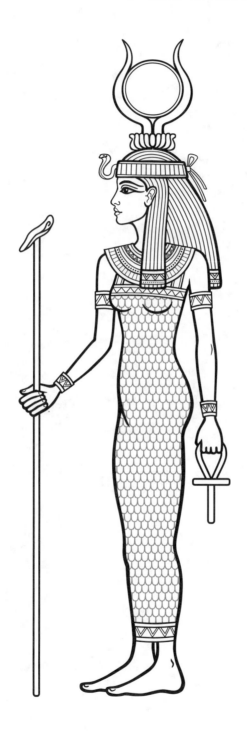

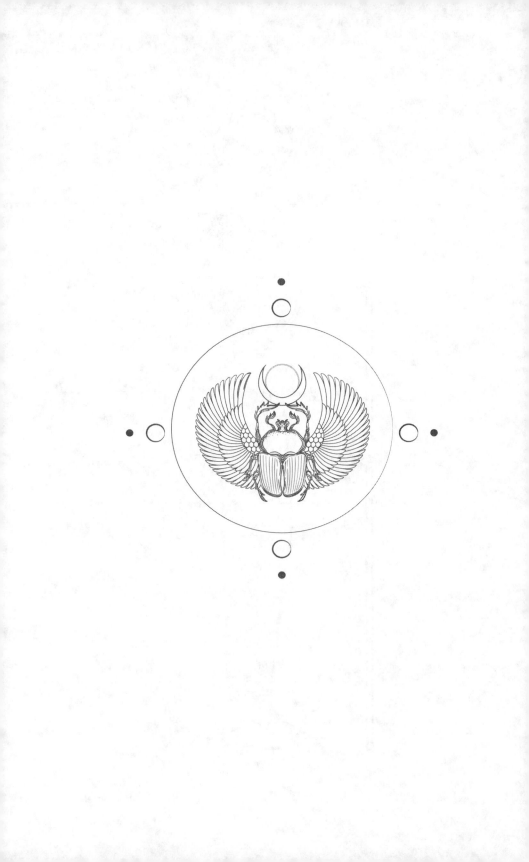

Epagomenae and The Game of Passing

*K*honsu the Moon laid out the senet tokens. He slid out the drawer of blue-glazed pieces, the pawns tinkling softly. He arranged them—*five and five*—on the thirty tiles of the board and considered what stakes he would lay on the game.

When the world was water, Ra sent his spirit in the shape of a phoenix to fly over the abyss. The phoenix screamed and shattered the silence of chaos, and so the world was born. The same cry created Ma'at—order and rightness. Without Ma'at, all returns to the unmoving, barren water and the chaos-snake that still lurks in the depths of the Duat, the Underworld. Ra's eternal battle for Ma'at upholds everything.

As the world took form, Geb the Earth loved his sister the Sky, and divine child after divine child sprang up in her womb of Heaven, threatening the entire sphere of creation. What could these children bring but change? What could they be formed of, if not power? Great power unsettles all things, and so Ra forbade their births. In defense of Ma'at, he separated Earth from Sky, Geb from Nut. He turned his bright face to the Goddess whose body is the Cover of the Sky, to the One Who Protects, and declared that she could not give birth on any day of the year. In his perfect round of 360 days, Ra the Lord of the Wheel would not allow it.

Khonsu the Pathfinder smiled as he prepared to receive guests. Sopdet— the brightest star in the sky—had risen, but the Black Land remained dry. The new year's flood waters had not yet swollen over the fields, and the land of Kemet was between times.

In the heaviness of five simultaneous pregnancies, Nut grieved. She turned to Thoth, the Lord of Time who loved her. He reckons the years, each heb (festival) a notch on his staff. But Thoth did not have the power to make days. The light of the Sun is Ra's alone.

Khonsu the Timekeeper saw the approaching Opening of the Year, prepared for the heb of Wepet-Renpet. When the waters rise, feasting, dancing and drinking follow, but first Kemet sings the lamentation for Wsjr, for the fallen king revived by magic even in death. Life follows death, and renewal flows from it as the river flows over the stubs of last year's grain. Khonsu the Traveler tracks his course above it all.

Gravid Nut carried her children day upon day until the end of the year, but there was hope in her heart. She looked down on the body of her husband the Earth. No swollen river yet drowned the fields. Shemu the harvest-time had come and gone, but until the water appeared, it was not yet the season of Akhet. It was a time between.

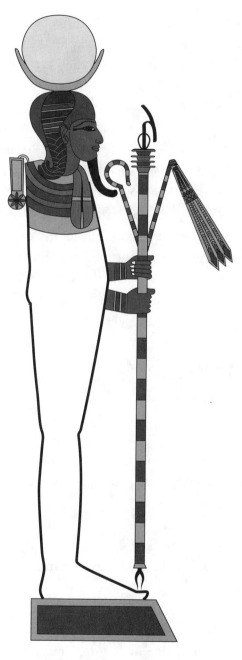

Khonsu the Pathfinder

It is unlucky to linger between two things, so wise Thoth took Nut to visit Khonsu Who Drives Away Evil Spirits, to pass the time safely in games and talk. When they arrived, the table was laid and the pieces were already set out, and so the Gods played senet, the game of passing.

Khonsu the Greatest God of the Great Gods chose to bet what was only his to give: moonlight. He wouldn't bet much, though, because light is precious, and he could not defy the word of life-giving Ra.

Khonsu Decider of the Lifespan bet one seventieth part of his light— the merest sliver—and lost. He bet again and lost. Over and over he bet and played and lost until enough moonlight for five days was handed over. Nut smiled at her winnings and rose, ungainly, from the table.

Who can know how Nut and Thoth won so many rounds, how Khonsu allowed so much of his light to slip from his hands? Who can guess what the hearts of the immortal Gods might hold?

In her birthing chamber of stolen time, black-haired Nut brought forth the Gods:

On the first day, she birthed you, Wsjr,
Great King Osiris who rules the Duat!

On the second day, she brought you forth, Heru-ur,
Horus-on-the-Horizon with your right eye the star of morning
and your left the star of evening!

She brought you into the light, Desert Lord Sutekh.
Slayer of Apep, each night you protect Ra from the
serpent of chaos!

On the fourth day the Mother of Gods gave birth to you,
Weret-Kekau, sistrum-ringing Isis, the Great Magic!

On the fifth day, Nut brought you forth Nebet-het,
Nephthys the Friend of the Dead!
At twilight the people pray to you,
Mistress of the House of Heaven,
that Seth will hold back Apep in the night!

May he defeat the serpent so that Ra
may rise as Khepri in the morning,
and sail his Boat of Millions of Years
across the sky!

Millions of years may Ra shine on the Earth!
Millions of years may the Gods fight for Ra
as he travels nightly through the Duat!
May Ra uphold Ma'at—truth and order—forever!

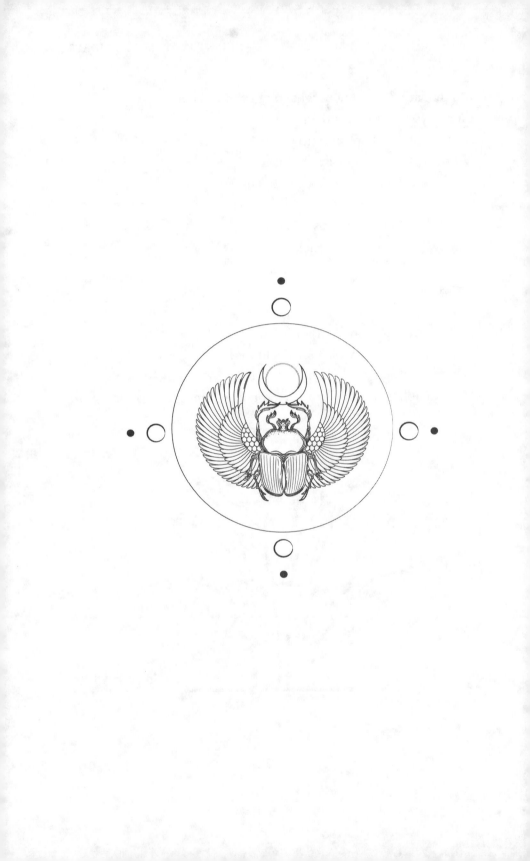

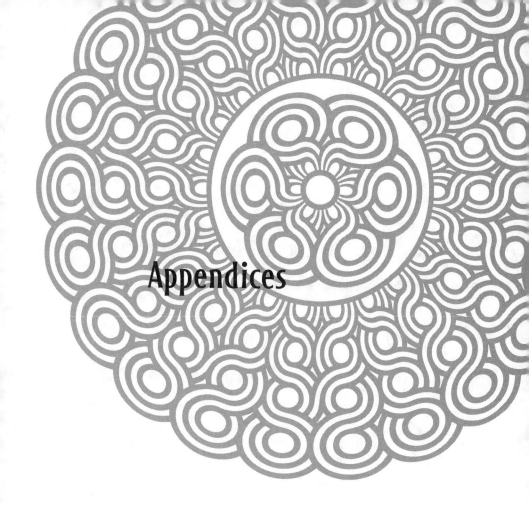

Appendices

Appendix I
Egyptian God Names

Thoth	Djehuty	
Hapi	Hpy	
Ra	Re	
Amun	Jmn/Imn	
Isis	Aset	
Nephthys	Nebet-Het	
Osiris	Wsjr	
Seth	Setekh	

Tefnut	Tefnut	
Sekhmet	Sikma	
Hathor	Hut-hor	
Ma'at	M't	
Khepri	Hprj	
Ptah	Pth	
Bast	B'stjt	
Horus	Heru	
Min	Mnw	

Nut	Nwt	
Geb	Geb	
Shu	Sw	
Anubis	Anpu	

Appendix II
Table of New Moon Dates for Min and Wadi Festivals

Year	Min New Moon between March 16–April 14	Wadi New Moon between April 15–May 14
2022	April 1	April 30
2023	March 21	April 20
2024	April 8	May 8
2025	March 29	April 27
2026	March 19	April 17
2027	April 6	May 6
2028	March 26	April 24
2029	April 13	May 13
2030	April 2	May 2
2031	March 23	April 21
2032	April 10	May 9
2033	March 30	April 29
2034	March 20	April 18
2035	April 8th	May 7
2036	March 27	April 26
2037	March 16	April 15
2038	April 4	May 4
2039	March 24	April 23
2040	April 11	May 11

Appendix III
Festivals by Associated Deities

AMUN

Amun-Ra is the netjer of the month of Rekehnedjes.
Opet Festival—15th–26th of Menkhet
Amun in the Festival of Raising Heaven—30th of Rekehwer
Return of the statue of Amun—1st of Rekehnedjes
Wadi, the Beautiful Feast of the Valley—New Moon in Khentkhety
Offerings to Hapi and Amun to secure a good flood—15th
    of Ipet-Hemet

ANUBIS

Adoration of Anubis—10th of Khonsu

BAST

Day of Chewing Onions for Bast—4th of Renenutet

THE DEAD

Wag Festival—18th of Thoth
Wadi, the Beautiful Feast of the Valley—New Moon in Khentkhety

THE ENNEAD

Festival of Osiris and the Ennead—5th of Menkhet
Khoiak Festival—18th–30th of Khoiak

HAPI

Hapi is the netjer of the season of Akhet.
Offerings to Hapi and Amun to secure a good flood—15th
    of Ipet-Hemet

HATHOR

Hathor is the netjer of the month of Hathor.
Tekh Festival—20th of Thoth
Festival of Hathor—1st of Khoiak
Wadi, the Beautiful Feast of the Valley—New Moon in Khentkhety

HORUS

Horus is the netjer of the month of Khentkhety and Heru–Khuiti is
the netjer of the month of Wepet-renpet.

ISIS

Wepet-renpet Festival—1st of Thoth
Feast of Isis—6th of Hathor
Lamentations of Isis and Nephthys—17th of Hathor
Khoiak—Raising the Djed Pillar—30th of Khoiak
Festival of Isis—2nd of Wepet-renpet

KHEPRI

Khepri is the netjer of the season of Peret.

KHONSU

Khonsu-Ra is the netjer of the season of Shemu and the
    month of Khonsu.
Wadi, the Beautiful Feast of the Valley—New Moon in Khentkhety
Epagomenal Days

MA'AT

Festival of Ma'at—21st of Hathor

MIN

Min is the netjer of the month of Shefbedet.
Festival of Min—New moon in Khonsu

MUT

Wadi, the Beautiful Feast of the Valley—New Moon in Khentkhety

NEHEBKAU

Nehebkau Festival—1st of Shefbedet

NEITH

Neith, the Festival of Lamps—13th of Ipet-Hemet

NEPHTHYS

Wepet-renpet Festival—1st of Thoth

Lamentations of Isis and Nephthys—17th of Hathor

Khoiak—Raising the Djed Pillar—30th of Khoiak

NEPRI

Festival of Renenutet and birth of Nepri—1st of Khonsu

NUT

Epagomenal Days

OSIRIS

Wepet-renpet Festival—1st of Thoth

Wag Festival—18th of Thoth

Wag and Thoth Festival—19th of Thoth

Procession of Osiris—22nd of Thoth

Festival of Osiris and the Ennead—5th of Menkhet

Khoiak Festival—18th–30th of Khoiak

Khoiak—Ploughing the Earth—22nd of Khoiak

Khoiak—Solar Festival—26th of Khoiak

Khoiak—Raising the Djed Pillar—30th of Khoiak

Nehebkau—1st of Shefbedet

PTAH

Ptah is the netjer of the month of Menkhet.

Festival of Ptah—1st of Rekehnedjes

REKHUR

Rekhur is the netjer of the month of Rekehwer.

RENENUTET

Renenutet is the netjer of the month of Renenutet.

Harvest offering to Renenutet—25th of Renenutet

Granary offering to Renenutet—27th of Renenutet

Festival of Renenutet and birth of Nepri—1st of Khonsu

SEKHMET

Sekhmet is the netjer of the month of Khoiak.

Tekh Festival—20th of Thoth

SHENTAYIT

Khoiak—Ploughing the Earth—22nd of Khoiak

SOKAR

Khoiak—Sokar Festival—26th of Khoiak

THOTH

Thoth is the netjer of the month of Thoth.

Wag and Thoth Festival—19th of Thoth

WADJET

Wadjet is the netjer of the month of Ipet-Hemet.

WEPWAWET

Khoiak Festival—18th–30th of Khoiak

Appendix IV
Ancient Egyptian Historical Overview

This book refers to various periods to date certain practices or ritual texts. The developments, zeitgeist and major events of each era are briefly described below. While the differences between periods are real, bear in mind always that one of ancient Egypt's most notable features was its cultural constancy. Egypt's long history winds through time like the Nile, expanding and receding as the region was unified and then separated, unified and then separated, unified and then conquered. Throughout all, Egypt was extraordinarily stable. Government never totally collapsed—rather it retreated to the local level. Through famines, invasions and political upsets, there was never a dark age in Egypt.

While Egypt might go to war and might engage in trade, it was always primarily an agricultural society. Seats of power might shift from one city to another, over the centuries one God might gain ascendancy over another, but the daily journey of the Sun and the reliable rhythm of the waters rising and falling with the annual inundation remained the steady twin heartbeats of the country.

The various eras of Egyptian history are called Kingdoms when the nation is united and Periods when it is not. These are names assigned by modern historians and not distinctions the ancient Egyptians themselves made.

Predynastic Period
5000 BCE – 3150 BCE

There was farming and herding in Egypt as early as 8000 BCE. The development of agriculture and the domestication of animals did not happen exclusively in the Nile Valley but were part of the Neolithic Agricultural Revolution. This period is marked by a shift to settled agriculture and herding that was concurrent with the domestication of various grains by hunter-gatherers who bred them for qualities that made them easier to harvest. This happened in many places independently across the world within a relatively short period. In Egypt, the main crops were emmer and einkorn wheat and barley, but in other regions of the world rice, maize, squash, lentils, peas, chickpeas and vetch were domesticated around the same time. Some of these spread

from the Near East to Egypt and quickly became staple foods there as well.

For the most part, the land in Egypt in this period was still very dry and people were generally nomadic until beginning to settle along the Nile around 6000 BCE. The earliest reference to irrigation is in 3100 BCE, but there was likely some organized ditch irrigation before that date. As they settled, people grouped themselves in villages which became towns and then cities. These became city-states called *nomes*. These were originally autonomous but slowly developed into the two kingdoms of Upper and Lower Egypt.

Much of what is typically Egyptian was developed in this period before the unification of the country. There are faience workshops dating to 5500 BCE, indicating that even the earliest Egyptians—like their descendants—valued beauty and adornment. By 4500 BCE, people were buried with possessions and offerings. There were mummies and tombs to house them by 3500 BCE and hieroglyphic writing was developed around 3300 BCE. There was red and black pottery and jewelry, weapons and artwork decorated with copper, silver, gold and lapis, the precious materials from which later statues of the Gods would be crafted. Egyptian religion was also a feature of the predynastic period. Not only did the burial practices increasingly indicate belief in an afterlife, but each city had local zoomorphic deities whose relationships and alliances shifted with human politics and wars.

Early Dynastic Period
3150 BCE–2613 BCE
Dynasty 1–Dynasty 3

MAJOR TEXTS AND ARTIFACTS:
The Narmer Palette, Step Pyramid

In 3150 BCE, a king of wealthy Upper Egypt conquered Lower Egypt, unifying the country for the first time. This first king—the title of pharaoh was not yet in use—was Narmer, whose name translates to "raging catfish." He is also probably the king who bore the title Menes, which means "the one who endures." His conquest is recorded on the Narmer Palette, on one side of which he is shown wearing the white Hedjet crown of Upper Egypt and wielding a mace to kill captive soldiers while on the other side he

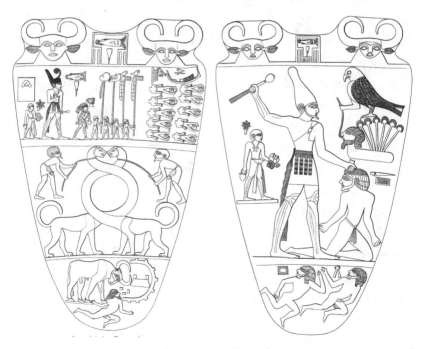

Narmer Pallet

wears the red Deshret crown of Lower Egypt in a royal procession to inspect the decapitated bodies of his slaughtered victims.

Narmer ruled from several cities, one of them Memphis. It is from Memphis that Egypt derives its English name—first from the Greek *Aegyptos*, which is a Hellenized transliteration of *hwt-ka-Ptah*, the name of Memphis which means, "the house of the soul of Ptah." The Egyptians called their country *Kemet*—the Black Land, referring to the precise boundary of the red desert sand and the rich, black soil left behind by the annual flood.

To consolidate his power, Narmer married a princess from the formidable city of Naqada, Neithhotep. When she died, her tomb was just as richly decorated as a king's would have been, so she likely wielded great personal authority rather than being simply a treaty wife. Under their rule Egypt conquered territory to the East and the South and undertook large-scale building projects. Cities became larger as well, and their descendants ruled for several generations.

In the second dynasty that followed them, kings first began to use the names of Gods in association with their own names, laying the groundwork for the later cult of the king as divine king. Until the middle of the second dynasty, the king was related primarily with Horus. A king named Peribsen, however, chose to instead associate his name with that of Set, perhaps a political move as the cult of Horus was focused in Lower Egypt.

During the first two dynasties, tombs became larger and more elaborate. These rectangular mudbrick or stone structures were called *mastabas*—a word meaning "house of eternity"—which were a precursor to pyramids. In the third dynasty—sometimes assigned to the Old Kingdom period—Peribsen's grandson Djoser built the first pyramid. An innovation of the architect Imhotep, this step pyramid resembled the previous mastaba tombs, but stacked one atop the next to form the massive structure. Imhotep did not just design the first pyramid, though. He oversaw the construction of an entire complex of temples associated with it, surrounded by a massive wall with thirteen false doors and only one real one. This trickiness extended to the temples as well—the Northern Mortuary Temple contains a secret entrance to the pyramid.

These temples included columns with no architectural function, that is, they did not play a part in supporting the walls or roofs and were purely decorative. Although the temples were constructed from stone, most buildings in Egypt at that time were made of mudbrick—unfired brick. It is a comparatively weak building material and bundles of river reeds supported and propped up the walls. It is these reeds that the stone columns represent, evoking stability even when the walls and roof don't need them. Thousands of years later, columns still serve this function as they are most

Stepped Pyrmaid of Sakkarra

commonly found on institutions known for or striving for stability—banks, schools, churches, courts and other government buildings. These all have an interest in conveying the ideas of solidity, permanence and immovable strength.

These first three dynasties saw many important developments in Egyptian life, likely because of the stability brought about through centralized government. There were agricultural advances, the development of the calendar and rapid refinements in art and architecture, seen first and foremost in the construction of the first pyramid. The religious concept of *ma'at*—harmonious order—became prominent. At the same time, the belief in and valuing of an eternal life after death—moderated through funeral cults—was amplified.

Old Kingdom
2613 BCE – 2181 BCE
Dynasty 4–Dynasty 6

MAJOR TEXTS AND ARTIFACTS:
The pyramid texts, pyramids, the sphinx

Ruled from Memphis during this period, Egypt became very wealthy, and with wealth comes power. The bureaucratic functions of government were refined, and it is this bureaucracy that kept Egypt so stable for millenia. The Old Kingdom is the era of pyramid building, particularly under the kings Sneferu, Khufu, Khafre and Menkaure. These last three are the Giza pyramids and it is these—along with other monuments of the period—that provide the best historical records of the Old Kingdom, literally carved in stone.

Each pyramid, temple and monument required thousands of workers to construct over multiple decades—Khufu's pyramid, for example, contained nearly six million pounds of limestone and was built over twenty years. This indicates a powerful central authority and a bureaucracy that was both efficient and effective. Contrary to the popular image promoted by Hollywood, the pyramids were not built by slave labor unless you consider the average Egyptian worker a slave. While slavery did exist in ancient Egypt—and was as cruel and dehumanizing there as anywhere else—slaves were war captives and primarily labored in the mines. The pyramids were constructed by farmers and other workers who were employed as builders during the flood season when the water covered their fields. Some of the graffiti on Khufu's pyramid reveals that one of the groups of workers called themselves "the craftsmen gang." Other groups had names such as "the vigorous gang" and "the enduring gang."

Rather than relying on taxes, the kings directly owned the majority of farmland. They employed individuals and served as a method of redistributing wealth. Estates rather than individuals were taxed, and these estates were owned by the kings but managed by royal officials or temples who employed local people to work them and were responsible for seeing that the profit from them was turned over to the kings. Taxes were collected in kind, usually grain, herd animals and fabric. These were collected by the crown and then redistributed as payment for building projects and upkeep of various divine and funerary cults. In this way, large construction projects fueled the economy and supported the people in the agricultural off season. However well it provided for the average Egyptian, it was at heart a feudal system, but not one that produced an oppressed peasant class—workers were well paid, provided with health care and were known to go on strike.

The Fourth Dynasty king Sneferu associated kingship directly with Ra and under the reign of his grandson Djedefre, kings were referred to as sons of Ra, a step downward in power. During the Fifth Dynasty the solar cult was mediated by the priests and not the kings, with the priests of Ra continually gaining more power. As the kingship weakened, the *nomarchs*—rulers of the city-state provinces that made up the original political units of Egypt—became more powerful and together with the priesthood, they significantly weakened the central government.

During the Fifth Dynasty, the spells of the Pyramid Texts were written. These texts were carved inside the subterranean tomb of the Fifth Dynasty king Unas as well as subsequent kings. They provide the best depiction of Egyptian religion in the Old Kingdom and are the oldest Egyptian religious texts. They include many types of protective and mortuary spells but their primary purpose is to guide the soul of the dead king out of the tomb and to the afterlife. Entreating the soul to leap, jump and fly from the tomb, they include pleas and even threats to the Gods. They associate the king with both Osiris and Ra—even entreating the deceased king to sit on the throne of Osiris—marking a shift toward associating the kingship with the cult of Osiris. The Fifth Dynasty kings tend to have Ra in their names and are called the Sun Kings, so the prominent role of Osiris in the Pyramid Texts signals a meaningful departure from the prior dominance of Ra.

By the Sixth Dynasty, as priesthoods and local governments continued to gain more power and centralized leadership of Egypt faltered, leading to the First Intermediate Period. The last ruler of the Fifth Dynasty, Pepi II, ascended to the throne at six years old and ruled for 90 years. During his reign, foreign policy suffered and there was little diplomacy between Egypt and other nations. Scenes of warfare during his reign appear to be copies of earlier works and are probably symbolic rather than historical. The life-bringing floods were not as good during this period, farming suffered and famine was widespread. Nobles were gaining power but losing loyalty to the king. The king Pepi II created two vizier roles for the two parts of the country—Upper and Lower, signaling a weakening unification. Egypt was starving and its great wealth was dwindling. A king in an unprosperous country is not king for long, and while Pepi II survived the misfortunes of his reign, the dynasty did not. On his death, the government collapsed and the halves of Egypt split from each other.

Khafre Enthroned

First Intermediate Period
2181 BCE–2040 BCE
Dynasty 7–Dynasty 11

MAJOR TEXTS AND ARTIFACTS:
The Coffin Texts, The Lamentations of Isis and Nephthys

Nomarchs stepped into the power vacuum left by the weakened kings and during this period, provinces ruled themselves. Ineffectual nobles claiming descent from Pepi II still claimed to rule from Memphis and even received some taxes, while Herakliopolis was the seat of the Ninth and Tenth Dynasties and the Thebes the seat of the Eleventh Dynasty. But none of these exerted much power outside their local areas until the Eleventh Dynasty king who reunified Egypt—Menuhotep I.

The First Intermediate Period was a time of social as well as governmental upheaval. Wealth was no longer concentrated in the kingship and ordinary people could now afford better homes and luxuries such as decorative gardens, statuary and fine pottery. Some of these items were mass produced rather than lovingly crafted by a single artisan, resulting in a general overall decline in the quality of art, but an uptick in quantity and access to it.

During the Old Kingdom, artistic and architectural standards were set by the state and were very strict. With the weakening of authority in the First Intermediate Period, there was more artistic license and the styles of each region differed more from one another, including in the depictions of the Gods.

One of the major religious development that comes from this period is the idea that ordinary people could attain an eternal afterlife rather than just the kings and their immediate families. Average people in this period could afford tomb inscriptions—these were called Coffin Texts and served the same function as the Pyramid Texts, but for the ordinary person. The deceased person would see them when they awoke in their tomb and remember themselves. They guide the soul through a purifying fire that surrounds the body of Osiris, restoring and emancipating whoever passes through it. The Coffin Texts include *The Book of Two Ways*, which are the earliest maps in the world—maps of the afterlife lest the deceased get lost.

The spells of the Coffin Texts are intertwined with the myths of Osiris far more than are the Pyramid Texts. The cult of Osiris gained popularity and prominence during this era. The First of the Westerners—a reference to the setting Sun as a symbol of death—he had died, been revived by magic and then gained an eternal life, and he offered this same renewed life to those who believed in him. *The Lamentations of Isis and Nephthys* is a call and response song in which women take on the roles of the two sisters as they chant spells to revive Osiris. This was performed at individual funerals as well as at festivals of Osiris, and offered participants a share in the spiritual death and rebirth of the God.

Old Kingdom Tomb Saqara

In the worldview of the balance of ma'at, the king was essential to Egypt's order and harmony and so the freedom of the First Intermediate Period gave way to a return to centralized power. The first king of the Eleventh Dynasty, Intef I, began to challenge the Herakliopolitan kings. His successor Menuhotep I proclaimed that Thebes was the only true capital in the country. He began conquering the nomes, work which was continued by his successors. One by one, they were united under the rule of the Eleventh Dynasty. Wahankh Intef II conquered Abydos—the site of the tombs of the early kings. With this act, he claimed his right to rule the entire country as the early kings had done. He was resisted by the kings in Herakliopolis but in addition to fighting them throughout his reign, he also took on the responsibilities of the earlier kings, building temples, restoring monuments and upholding ma'at in his laws, judgments and policies. He consolidated power fiercely, so that the nomarchs who ruled under him wielded far less power than they had become accustomed to. His son followed in his footsteps and his grandson Mentuhotep II finally conquered Herakliopolis, reuniting Egypt and earning the title "a second Menes."

Middle Kingdom
2040 BCE–1782 BCE
Dynasty 11–13

With central authority in Thebes restored, the kings returned to their patronage of the arts, with craftsmen surpassing previous standards. This was due in part to access to materials through trade, as Egypt was increasingly wealthy. The unifier Mentuhotep II's son Mentuhotep III sent ships to Punt in the South for resins, gold, ivory and ebony.

The Middle Kingdom is generally considered a golden age of Egyptian art and literature. This artistic revival was not just a return to the cultural standards, principles and practices of the Old Kingdom, but a reimagining and reorganization of them. National cohesion was emphasized—unity was a form of order, an upholding of ma'at. New forms of literature appeared, including narrative stories whereas the Old Kingdom texts were primarily religious or practical. Art also began to incorporate images of daily life—scenes of hunting and fishing and landscapes. These were typically in tombs and served a religious purpose of reminding the soul of the deceased of the beauty of life. Monumental sculptures were common and figures became more life-like, even to the point of showing the age and weariness of the king, unthinkable under the idealized standards of the Old Kingdom.

Pyramid architecture, however, suffered. Middle Kingdom rulers constructed pyramids, but placed a limestone façade on a mudbrick core, most of which have crumbled to dust on the desert floor while the Old Kingdom pyramids remain. Few temples from this period have survived, either.

The priesthood of Amun continued to become more influential throughout the Middle Kingdom. Osiris had become prominent during the First Intermediate Period and in the Middle Kingdom he gained true ascendancy in the religion of the people, appearing as judge of the dead.

Mentuhotep II as Osiris

While Amun's worship was focused at Thebes, the cult of Osiris was at Abydos, where in legend the God's head had been buried. The temples there became sites of pilgrimage for worshippers of Osiris.

Despite the widespread prosperity of the period, ordinary people apparently felt the need to curse their neighbors fairly regularly. Egyptian curses are clay objects with a person's name and spells written on them to recite before smashing the object. When it is destroyed, so is the enemy whose name it bore. There are far more of these curse objects during the Middle Kingdom than other eras.

The first king of the Twelfth Dynasty, Amenemhet I, left Thebes and shifted the capital to Itjtawy. His successor Senusret I undertook building projects such as an Old Kingdom ruler might have done. He began the construction of the Karnak temple complex with a temple to Amun, a sign of Amun's rising power within the religion of Egypt. Senusret III was a great military victor who expanded Egypt's territory into the ancient kingdom of Nubia to the South (in modern Sudan.) His son Amenemhet III emphasized diplomacy, augmenting Egypt's already great wealth.

Beginning with Amenemhet I, the monarchy deliberately reduced the power of the nomarchs by removing them from control of the military. Previously, it was the task of the nomarch to send soldiers to the king to serve in the army, but Amenemhet I claimed direct control of the army himself. By the rein of Senusret III, nomarchs no longer held positions of much, if any, authority, and the title vanishes. The family names of former nomarchs, however, appear in records as various administrators in the royal government, and are often accompanied by tales of their great loyalty to the king, indicating a relationship of mutual appeasement. Claiming more direct control over the provinces removed the political barriers to the king's authority, resulting in improved roads, extensive building projects, and the construction of irrigation canals that increased agricultural production by making more water available to more people.

The Twelfth Dynasty saw the kingship held within the family of Amenemhet I for 200 years. They maintained their control through the practice of co-regency, in which the king would rule alongside his son or other chosen younger successor, who would then immediately take full control upon the death of the elder. Egypt's first historically probable queen ruled in the Twelfth Dynasty, Sobekneferu, sister or perhaps wife of Amenemhet IV, who had no sons. She is depicted as fully female, unlike the later Hatshepsut who is given masculine features. She also died without an heir, ending the Twelfth Dynasty.

In contrast to the Twelfth, the Thirteenth Dynasty was unstable. A number of kings ruled for less than a year, and the succession of the kingship itself became less reliant on kinship and was passed around among noble families rather than being held by a single family. Many royal tombs were left unfinished. Most importantly, the Hyksos people began to take control of Lower Egypt during the Thirteenth Dynasty and the kings were not able to stop them.

Relief of Nebhepetre MentuhotepII

Second Intermediate Period
1782 BCE–1570 BCE
Dynasty 13–Dynasty 17

There were three seats of power in Egypt during this period. The Thirteenth Dynasty relocated the capital to Thebes and ruled from there. At the time of the Sixteenth Dynasty in Thebes, the Hyksos ruled as the Fifteenth from Avaris in the North and the Nubians in the South, who called their territory the kingdom of Kush.

The Hyksos—like so many conquerors after them—maintained the traditions and religion of Egypt, adapting to their new country rather than imposing their own ways on it. Their identity is unclear, but the strong trade relations of the Middle Kingdom brought many people from the Levant to the Delta region. *Hyksos* is simply a Greek transliteration of an Egyptian phrase meaning "kings of foreign lands."

The Nubians were long trading partners of the Egyptians, and were familiar with Egyptian religion and customs. They took these on for themselves when ruling in the South so that Kush was in most ways culturally Egyptian.

Relations and trade between these rulers were peaceful until the Seventeenth Dynasty. Seqenenra Ta'O of Thebes received a message from Apepi at Avaris telling him to move his hippopotamus pool because it was too noisy. Ta'O responded to this insult by attacking Avaris and he died in the battle. His son Kamose continued his war until his death and was succeeded by his brother Ahmose I. After several more battles at Avaris, Ahmose I succeeded in driving the Hyksos out of Egypt, pursuing them to Palestine and laying siege to them there so that they eventually fled to Syria. After returning to Egypt, Ahmose I turned his attention to the South, reconquering the territory which had been lost to Kush.

During the Second Intermediate Period, the ability to compose hieroglyphic writing was diminished and hieratic script was developed. There were cultural gains for Egypt in the cross-pollination, however. Many improvements to weapons come from this period and most importantly, knowledge of the chariot.

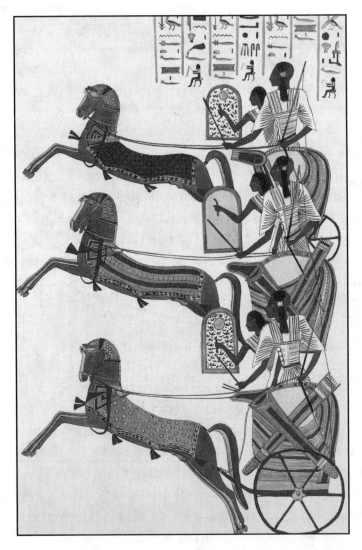

Illustration of chariots from the Rosalini expedition
into the tomb of Ramses III

New Kingdom
1570 BCE–1069 BCE
Dynasty 18–Dynasty 20

MAJOR TEXTS AND ARTIFACTS:
The Book of Going Forth by Day (The Book of the Dead)

Ahmose I's conquests led to a nationalistic sensibility. The rulers and people of Egypt wanted most of all to prevent another foreign invasion, and this was the impetus for the conquests of the New Kingdom. The first pharaohs of the period simply wanted to create a buffer zone between Egypt and other nations, but by Thuthmose III, the desire to maintain independence had evolved into imperial aspirations and Egypt began to build an empire.

The rulers of the New Kingdom were pharaohs—previous kings were simply kings. The new title meant "great house." The pyramids of the Old Kingdom dominate the popular image of Egypt, but the apex of Egyptian culture was the New Kingdom. Ahmose I's son Amenhotep I was also warlike, but is best known for his patronage of the arts, particularly for supporting the craftsmen in the Valley of the Kings. It is also under his rule that *The Book of Going Forth by Day (The Book of the Dead)* was finalized. This text of spells provides a richly illustrated guide to the Underworld, with the Hall of Judgment and the weighing of the soul against the feather of Ma'at. Literacy generally was far more widespread than in earlier eras, with ordinary people even sending personal letters.

After Amenhotep I, his successor Thuthmose I expanded Egypt's territory in Nubia, Syria and the Levant. His daughter Hatshepsut was his designated successor, and after the brief rule of her brother, she became one of the greatest New Kingdom pharaohs. She was best known for her vast building projects, but later pharaohs removed her name from her buildings and monuments and claimed them as their

Passage from *The Book of theDead* for the singer of Amun.

own. After her, Thuthmose III was the pharaoh who truly built an empire for Egypt, conquering territory in every direction. His success was due in part to the technologies learned from the Hyksos—bronze weapons and the chariot.

The pharaohs of the New Kingdom continued to gain power and wealth, ruling in unprecedented opulence. However much the pharaoh owned, though, the priests of Amun owned more. To check the power of the priesthood, Amenhotep IV attempted to drastically alter Egyptian religion, replacing Amun with Aten—the disk of the Sun. He made this change in his own name as well and ruled as Akhenaten during this brief period of strange monotheism.

Akhenaten abolished worship of other Gods beside Aten and upended the religious power structure and its symbolic paradigm. He also moved the capital from Thebes to Amarna. He placed his new city—named after himself—on the West bank of the Nile, the side of death and the dying Sun, as if to prove that bad luck from the old theology could not harm him. The art style of his reign is soft and fluid, a clear contrast to the rigidity of most traditional Egyptian art. His wife was Nefertiti and her famous bust exemplifies this Amarna art style.

While Akhenaten's religious reforms might have been a bold political move, they did not have a lasting impact on the religious expression of the nation. His son Tutankhaten immediately changed his name to Tutankhamun. He moved the capital from Amarna to Memphis and re-opened the temples. After his death at eighteen years of age, his wife and half sister attempted to rule alone but was quickly put aside by the powerful general Horemheb. Once on the throne, Horemheb removed the Amarna period from history to the best of his ability, destroying monuments of Akhenaten and removing his name from inscriptions by chipping it out of the stone.

Horemheb returned Egypt to traditional polytheistic religion and restored stability, but he had no heir and was succeeded by Ramesses I, who had been his vizier. A great deal of territory had been lost under Akhenaten, so Ramesses immediately assigned his son Seti to reconquering it. When he died, Seti I continued the projects of restoration and revitalization undertaken by both his father and by Horemheb.

Seti I's son Ramesses II—called The Great—defeated the Hittites at the battle of Kadesh, in which chariots played a significant role and the first recorded peace treaty in the world was signed after this battle. He built a city at Avaris called Per-Ramesses and moved the capital from Thebes to this new site. This move would prove problematic as the absence of the pharaohs gave the priests of Amun at Thebes an opportunity to claim even more authority in their absence.

The Kings of the Nineteenth Dynasty were powerful but the Twentieth Dynasty Kings had difficulty maintaining Egypt's conquered territory and central rule at home. They also faced significant competition from the priesthood. This was made possible in part by a theological development—the association between Ra and the creator Atum in the God Amun rendered him king of the Gods. He both made the world and sustained creation and by extension, Egypt. Previously, the pharaoh had been the primary intercessory between the nation, the people and the Gods, but now the priests could step into that role, representing Amun on Earth as only the pharaoh had done before.

During the New Kingdom, oracles became increasingly prominent. Because the priests of Amun claimed direct contact with and knowledge of their God, the ordinary person could now seek out his advice directly from them. It is during this period when the statue of the God would embark from the temple in its boat, carried by the priests, during festivals. The motions of the boat were interpreted as oracular answers to questions.

Akhenaten may have been rash in his actions, but the threat to the power of the kings posed by the priesthood of Amun was nonetheless real. At the time of the Twentieth Dynasty, they owned the majority of the land given to temples, as well as most of the ships and manufacturing organizations in Egypt. For three dynasties—Eighteen, Nineteen and Twenty—Egypt was as powerful as it had ever been on the foreign stage. At home, though, the priesthood of Amun was steadily gaining power at the expense of the pharaoh, with some priests even owning more land than the king. Eventually the priesthood openly asserted itself against the king, claiming the kingship and ruling from Thebes, leading to the Third Intermediate Period. After the death of Ramesses XI, his successor Smendes I buried him, claimed the throne and moved his capital to Tanis in Lower Egypt. His rule did not extend outside Lower Egypt, and his reign marks the end of the Twentieth Dynasty and the New Kingdom.

Third Intermediate Period
1069 BCE–525 BCE
Dynasty 21–Dynasty 25

A high priest of Amun named Herihor established a dynasty of priests in Thebes after the death of the last king of the Twentieth Dynasty while the Twenty-first Dynasty was ruling simultaneously from Tanis.

With Smendes I ruling much of Lower Egypt from Tanis, the priests of Amun ruling Upper Egypt from Thebes, the Nubians in the South took the opportunity to reclaim land they had lost at the beginning of the New Kingdom. Other parts of Egypt's empire did the same and soon, with no central government to hold them, Egypt lost control of all territories outside its own borders.

The rulers in Tanis were more traditional pharaohs—they consulted the Gods and then made their decisions. In contrast, the high priest in Thebes was an entirely theocratic ruler and the God was involved in every governmental decision, large or small. The relations between these rulers were marked by mutual respect and they would cooperate on policies and projects. At times, the two dynasties were related to one another as well.

The Twenty-second Dynasty—who were Libyan—continued in Tanis but Dynasties Twenty-three and Twenty-four shifted the capital first to Leontopolis and then to Sais. The New Kingdom was the last period during which Egypt was both united and self-ruling. The kings of the Kushite power of center of Napata in the South were allied with the priesthood of Amun and came into Egypt to recentralize the government, forming the Twenty-fifth Dynasty. Their power was checked by the invasion of the Assyrians, a furiously warlike nation who ruled an empire stretching from the Zagros Mountains to the Mediterranean Sea in the Levant. They

Stela of Herihor

invaded Egypt and sacked both Thebes and Memphis. Defeated by the Assyrians, the rulers of the Twenty-fifth dynasty retreated unceremoniously back to Napata.

During this period, there was cultural and religious continuity. The father-mother-son triads of Gods known from earlier eras, e.g., Amun, Mut and Khonsu, extended during this period to Isis, Osiris and Horus. The cult of Isis became particularly prominent and in later eras would go on to spread throughout the Mediterranean.

There were not many large-scale building projects without a central government to fund them, but the other arts thrived, and the Third Intermediate Period saw intricate artwork, especially painting, metalwork and statuary.

Late Period
525 BCE–332 BCE
Dynasty 26–Dynasty 31

Egypt did not remain long in the possession of Assyria—the Egyptians managed to drive the Assyrians out of the country under the leadership of a local ruler of Sais, Psamtik, establishing the Twenty-sixth Dynasty. The Assyrians were not the only conquering power of the era, though, and the Persians and Babylonians followed them.

When the Persians invaded under Cambyses II, the Persians had observed the Egyptians' reverence for the animals associated with their Gods. When they attacked the city of Pelusium, they painted Bast on their shields and rounded up all the cats and other stray animals before them in the battle. The Egyptians surrendered rather than offend Bast, but Cambyses staged a triumphal parade in which he had the cats thrown into the Egyptians' faces.

The Persians controlled Egypt throughout the rule of Cambyses II, but the Egyptians had some resistance. By the time of Cambyses' great-great nephew Darius II, the Egyptian Amyrtaeus was able to establish the Twenty-eighth Dynasty. He was the only king of that Dynasty, however, and he was followed by the Twenty-ninth Dynasty, ruling from Mendes. The Thirtieth Dynasty followed before the Persians regained control in 343 BCE, establishing themselves as Dynasty Thirty-one. After the main cities surrendered to him, the Persian king Artaxerxes III sacked all the temples, taking the loot back to Persia and imposing crippling taxes in Egypt.

The Persians were Zoroastrian monotheists and criminalized Egyptian religion, removing sacred texts even after the wealth of the temples had been looted. These strategies to dominate and subdue the country were effective—Egypt remained in the control of Persia until Alexander the Great conquered it for himself eleven years later.

Greco-Roman Period
332–30 BCE
Macedonian Kings and Ptolemaic Dynasty

Alexander the Great inherited his throne in Macedonia at the age of twenty and conquered the entire world as he knew it—from the River Ganges in the East to the border of modern Libya in the West—by thirty. Egypt was a crown jewel of that world and in 332 BCE Alexander was crowned King in the temple of Ptah in Memphis. A polytheist, Alexander built new temples to the Egyptian Gods and restored those that had been abandoned and neglected under Persian rule. He was considered something of a liberator and an oracle of Amun in the Siwa Oasis declared him the son of Amun. Some of Alexander's most famous iconography shows him with curling rams' horns protruding from his hair, a sign of his divinity as the ram was a sacred animal to Amun. Alexander himself considered Amun and Zeus to be a single deity and called Zeus-Amun his father. On his deathbed, he even requested that he be buried at the Siwa Oasis temple rather than in the Macedonian royal tombs or in Babylon where he fell ill.

Alexander ruled Egypt almost entirely in absentia, and after his sudden death in 323 his generals split the territory of his conquered empire amongst themselves, with Ptolemy taking Egypt for his own. To honor the wishes of Alexander and to establish himself as his true successor, Ptolemy stole Alexander's body while it was being transported back to Macedon, and he buried him in Egypt in Alexandria. Egypt continued under the rule of the Macedonian Ptolemies through seventeen of his descendants. The last of these was Cleopatra VII, who used all her wiles to keep Egypt from complete Roman rule, turning to seduction when war and wealth had failed. Her efforts bought Egypt sixteen more years of indepen-

Equestrian statue of Alexander the Great in Alexandria

dence and she bore four children to the rulers of Rome—one to Julius Caesar and three to Marc Antony. She supported Antony in his civil war against his rival Octavian (later Augustus) and when it was clear they had lost, both committed suicide in 30 BCE to avoid being shown off as prisoners in Octavian's victory parade. Believing Cleopatra had died first, Antony stabbed himself. Cleopatra used some kind of poison—tradition holds that she allowed herself to be bitten by an asp. Octavian (later Augustus) had Cleopatra's son with Caesar executed and the younger three taken to Rome, where he paraded them through the streets in chains of gold. He then placed them in the care of his sister—who was Marc Antony, their father's wife—and they disappeared from the historical record. They are generally presumed to have been murdered and Egypt became a Roman province.

Timeline

PREHISTORIC

6000 BCE settlements in the Nile Valley

6000 BCE faience workshop at Abydos

PREDYNASTIC PERIOD 5000–3150 BCE

Grid system for proportions developed

Painted pottery and figurines, cosmetic palettes

Upper and Lower Egypt

5000 BCE evidence of farming in Egypt

4000 BCE Gods appear on tomb wall art

3200 BCE hieroglyphic script developed

EARLY DYNASTIC 3150–2613 BCE

Memphis is the capital

3150 BCE unification of Upper and Lower Egypt by Menes

3100–3000 BCE approximate date of the Narmer Palette

2670 BCE the architect Imhotep builds the first pyramid
(Djoser's Pyramid)

OLD KINGDOM 2613–2181 BCE

Ra, Horus and Set are primarily associated with kingship

development of painting, first stelae, invention of potter's wheel

2560 BCE Khufu builds the Great Pyramid of Giza

2500 BCE the Sphinx of Giza is built

2400 BCE the Pyramid Texts

FIRST INTERMEDIATE PERIOD 2181–2040 BCE

Rule by Memphis in the North and Thebes in the South

Development of regional artistic styles
Rise of the cult of Osiris
Lamentations of Isis and Nephthys
2164 BCE Coffin Texts

MIDDLE KINGDOM 2040–1782 BCE
First obelisks
Osiris shown as judge of the dead
Amun becomes more influential with a cult center in Thebes
The king is shown as the child of a pair of Gods
1800 BCE Bronze working begins
1800 BCE Kahun Gynecological Papyrus addresses contraception

SECOND INTERMEDIATE PERIOD 1782–1570 BCE
Hieratic script developed
1700 BCE Kingdom of Kush founded

NEW KINGDOM 1570–1069 BCE
Abundance of art, briefly including the Amarna style
Valley of the Kings tombs constructed
Development of a middle class (artisans)
Cult of Amun becomes preeminent
1570 BCE Ahmose I defeats the Hyksos
1550 BCE The Book of Going Forth by Day
1504 BCE Egyptian empire reaches its greatest extent
1479–1458 BCE Reign of Queen Hatshepsut
1353–1357 BCE Reign of Akhenaten, the heretic king
1334 BCE Tutankhamun restores traditional religion
1279–1212 BCE Reign of Ramesses II, the Great
1274 BCE Battle of Kadesh between Ramessess II and the Hittites
1258 BCE Treaty of Kadesh, the first peace treaty in the world

THIRD INTERMEDIATE PERIOD 1069–525 BCE

Richly decorated statues with inlay

750 BCE Iron working begins in Egypt

712 BCE–671 BCE Rule by the Kushite dynasty

671 BCE Assyrians conquer Egypt

653 BCE Egyptians expel the Assyrians

601 BCE Babylon attacks, but does not conquer Egypt

LATE PERIOD 525–332 BCE

525 BCE Persia conquers Egypt

520 BCE Darius of Persia digs a canal to connect the Red Sea to the Nile River

GRECO-ROMAN PERIOD 332–30 BCE

331 BCE Alexander the Great conquers Egypt (the Egyptians do not resist)

331 BCE Alexander the Great founds Alexandria

323 BCE Death of Alexander the Great

323 BCE–282 BCE Reign of Ptolemy I Soter, who founded the Great Library

47 BCE Cleopatra VII becomes Queen of Egypt

43 BCE Temple of Isis and Serapis built in Rome

30 BCE Death of Cleopatra, Egypt becomes part of Roman Empire

Select Bibliograhy

Aldred, Cyril. *The Egyptians*. 3rd ed. London, UK: Thames & Hudson, 1998.

Allen, James P. *The Ancient Egyptian Pyramid Texts*. Atlanta, GA: SBL Press, 2015.

Baines, John, and Jaromír Málek. *Cultural Atlas of Ancient Egypt*. New York: Checkmate Books, 2000.

Baines, John, and Byron E Shafer. *Religion in Ancient Egypt: Gods, Myths, and Personal Practice*. London: Routledge, 1991.

Bleeker, C.J. *Egyptian Festivals*. BRILL, 2018.

Dennis, J T. *The Burden of Isis: Being the Laments of Isis and Nephtys*. Editorial: Murray, 1910.

Dosoo, Korshi. "Ancient Egyptian Religion." Oxford Research Encyclopedia of Religion, September 26, 2018. https://oxfordre.com/religion/display/10.1093/acrefore/9780199340378.001.0001/acrefore-9780199340378-e-246?rskey=RG0l7A&result=3.

Grajetzki, Wolfram, and Stephen Quirke. "Festivals in the Ancient Egyptian Calendar." Festivals in the Ancient Egyptian Calendar, 2003. https://www.ucl.ac.uk/museums-static/digitalegypt/ideology/festivaldates.html.

Hamlyn, Paul. *Egyptian Mythology*. London, UK: Paul Hamlyn, 1965.

Herodotus, Aubrey De Sélincourt, and John Marincola. *The Histories*. London, Penguin, 2003.

Hornung, Erik. *Idea into Image: Essays on Ancient Egyptian Thought*. Princeton, NJ: Timken Publishers, 1992.

Kaelin, Oskar. "Gods in Ancient Egypt." Oxford Research Encyclopedia of Religion, November 22, 2016. https://oxfordre.com/religion/display/10.1093/acrefore/9780199340378.001.0001/acrefore-9780199340378-e-244?rskey=RG0l7A&result=1.

Lesko, Leonard H. *Pharaoh's Workers: the Villagers of Deir El Medina*. Ithaca, Ny Cornell University Press, 2019.

Mark, Joshua J. "Ancient Egyptian Religion." World History Encyclopedia, January 20, 2016. https://www.worldhistory.org/Egyptian_Religion/.

Mercer, Samuel A. B. *The Pyramid Texts in Translation and Commentary*. Vol. 1. New York: Longmans, Green, 1952.

Pinch, Geraldine. *Egyptian Mythology: a Guide to the Gods, Goddesses, and Traditions of Ancient Egypt*. Oxford: Oxford University Press, 2004.

Plutarch, et al. *Greek Lives: A Selection of Nine Greek Lives*. New York, NY, Oxford University Press, 2019.

Redford, Donald B. *The Oxford Essential Guide to Egyptian Mythology*. New York, NY: Berkley Books, 2003.

Shaw, Ian. *The Oxford History of Ancient Egypt*. Toronto: C.N.I.B, 2006.

Szpakowska, Kasia. *Through a Glass Darkly: Magic, Dreams and Prophecy in Ancient Egypt*. Swansea: The Classical Press Of Wales, 2006.

Teeter, Emily. *Religion and Ritual in Ancient Egypt*. Cambridge: Cambridge University Press, 2011.

Wallis Budge, A. *Legends of the Eqyptian Gods*. Dover Publications, Inc, 1912, 1994

Literature of the Ancient Egyptians. J.M. Dent & Sons, Ltd, London, 1994

Watterson, Barbara. The House of Horus at Edfu: *Ritual in an Ancient Egyptian Temple*. Stroud: Tempus, 1998.

Ancient Roman Holidays by Mab Borden immerses readers in the sacred days, months and seasons of ancient Rome. Renowned for meticulous research and vivid descriptions, Borden unveils detailed accounts of revered deities and their ceremonial customs, emphasizes the profound significance of each. The book explains the ancient Roman calendar, detailing religious ritual activity and includes appendices that provide additional depth to the material presented in the book. Exploring festivals dedicated to Gods like Jupiter, Minerva and Bacchus, readers witness solemn processions and joyous celebrations. *Ancient Roman Holidays* invites readers to rediscover the beauty of these observances, revealing the traditions shaping the Roman calendar and immersing them in the vibrant tapestry of Roman spirituality and the sacred rhythms of life.

Ancient Greek Holidays by Mab Borden offers profound insights into the sacred days, months and seasons of ancient Greece. Renowned for meticulous research and vivid descriptions, Borden skillfully details each sacred day, revealing the honored deity and associated social and ritual activities. The book explains the interconnectedness between celestial rhythms and religious observances. Also included are appendices that enhance understanding. Readers journey through festivals dedicated to Gods such as Zeus, Athena and Apollo, gaining insights into the rituals, ceremonies and beliefs shaping ancient Greek spirituality. This book transports readers to a time when daily life was intricately connected to the divine, inspiring reflection on their own spiritual practices and inviting appreciation of the profound beauty of the sacred rhythms that shaped Greek society.

Come visit us at the
Witches' Almanac website

www.TheWitchesAlmanac.com

Aradia
Gospel of the Witches
Charles Godfrey Leland

ARADIA IS THE FIRST work in English in which witchcraft is portrayed as an underground old religion, surviving in secret from ancient Pagan times.

- Used as a core text by many modern Neo-Pagans.
- Foundation material containing traditional witchcraft practices
- This special edition features appreciations by such authors as Paul Huson, Raven Grimassi, Judika Illes, Michael Howard, Christopher Penczak, Myth Woodling, Christina Oakley Harrington, Patricia Della-Piana, Jimahl di Fiosa and Donald Weiser. A beautiful and compelling work, this edition is an up to date format, while keeping the text unchanged. 172 pages $16.95

The ABC of Magic Charms
Elizabeth Pepper

Mankind has sought protection from mysterious forces beyond mortal control. Humans have sought the help of animal, mineral, vegetable. The enlarged edition of *Magic Charms from A to Z*, guides us in calling on these forces. $12.95

The Little Book of Magical Creatures
Elizabeth Pepper and Barbara Stacy

AN UPDATE of the classic *Magical Creatures*, featuring Animals Tame, Animals Wild, Animals Fabulous—plus an added section of enchanting animal myths from other times, other places. *A must for all animal lovers.* $12.95

The Witchcraft of Dame Darrel of York
Charles Godfrey Leland, Introduction by Robert Mathiesen

A beautifully reproduced facsimile of the illuminated manuscript shedding light on the basis for a modern practice. A treasured by those practicing Pagans, as well as scholars.   Standard Hardcover $65.00 or Exclusive full leather bound, numbered and slipcased edition $145.00

DAME FORTUNE'S WHEEL TAROT: A PICTORIAL KEY
Paul Huson

Based upon Paul Huson's research in *Mystical Origins of the Tarot, Dame Fortune's Wheel Tarot* illustrates for the first time the earliest, traditional Tarot card interpretations as collected in the 1700s by Jean-Baptiste Alliette. In addition to detailed descriptions, full color reproductions of Huson's original designs for all 79 cards.

WITCHES ALL

A Treasury from past editions, is a collection from *The Witches' Almanac* publications of the past. Arranged by topics, the book, like the popular almanacs, is thought provoking and often spurs the reader on to a tangent leading to even greater discovery. It's perfect for study or casual reading,

GREEK GODS IN LOVE

Barbara Stacy casts a marvelously original eye on the beloved stories of Greek deities, replete with amorous oddities and escapades. We relish these tales in all their splendor and antic humor, and offer an inspired storyteller's fresh version of the old, old mythical magic.

MAGIC CHARMS FROM A TO Z

A treasury of amulets, talismans, fetishes and other lucky objects compiled by the staff of *The Witches' Almanac*. An invaluable guide for all who respond to the call of mystery and enchantment.

LOVE CHARMS

Love has many forms, many aspects. Ceremonies performed in witchcraft celebrate the joy and the blessings of love. Here is a collection of love charms to use now and ever after.

MAGICAL CREATURES

Mystic tradition grants pride of place to many members of the animal kingdom. Some share our life. Others live wild and free. Still others never lived at all, springing instead from the remarkable power of human imagination.

CELTIC TREE MAGIC

Robert Graves in *The White Goddess* writes of the significance of trees in the old Celtic lore. *Celtic Tree Magic* is an investigation of the sacred trees in the remarkable Beth-Luis-Nion alphabet and their role in folklore, poetry and mysticism.

MOON LORE

As both the largest and the brightest object in the night sky, and the only one to appear in phases, the Moon has been a rich source of myth for as long as there have been mythmakers.

MAGIC SPELLS
AND INCANTATIONS

Words have magic power. Their sound, spoken or sung, has ever been a part of mystic ritual. From ancient Egypt to the present, those who practice the art of enchantment have drawn inspiration from a treasury of thoughts and themes passed down through the ages.

LOVE FEASTS

Creating meals to share with the one you love can be a sacred ceremony in itself. With the Witch in mind, culinary adept Christine Fox offers magical menus and recipes for every month in the year.

RANDOM RECOLLECTIONS
III, IV

Pages culled from the original (no longer available) issues of *The Witches' Almanac,* published annually throughout the 1970s, are now available in a series of tasteful booklets. A treasure for those who missed us the first time around, keepsakes for those who remember.